"It took us over five years behind the bar to learn how to successfully navigate the minefields of romance. We would have given anything to have had Addickted on our bedside table! Kristina Grish offers the perfect cocktail for kicking that 'bad boy' habit we all seem to have."

Tracey Toomey and Leanne Shear
authors of *The Perfect Manhattan: A Novel*

"With no-holds-barred advice and enough laughs to make a good girl forget her bad boy ways, *Addickted* isn't just about kicking the habit, it's about kicking some ass along the way."

Jennifer O'Connell
author of *Bachelorette #1* and *Dress Rehearsal*

"Kristina Grish passionately deconstructs the allure of bad boys, and helps you evolve from 'hurts so good' to 'genuinely happy.'"

Nicole Beland,
author of *Girl Seeks Bliss*

ADDICKTED

12 STEPS TO KICKING YOUR BAD BOY HABIT

KRISTINA GRISH

POLKA DOT press™

AVON, MASSACHUSETTS

Published by Polka Dot Press,
an imprint of Adams Media, an F+W Publications Company
57 Littlefield Street, Avon, MA 02322
www.adamsmedia.com

ISBN 10: 1-59337-731-2
ISBN 13: 978-1-59337-731-1

Printed in the United States of America.

J   I   H   G   F   E   D   C   B   A

**Library of Congress Cataloging-in-Publication Data
is available from the publisher.**

This publication is designed to provide accurate and authoritative information
with regard to the subject matter covered. It is sold with the understanding that
the publisher is not engaged in rendering legal, accounting, or other professional
advice. If legal advice or other expert assistance is required, the services of a com-
petent professional person should be sought.
   —From a *Declaration of Principles* jointly adopted by a Committee of the
American Bar Association and a Committee of Publishers and Associations

Many of the designations used by manufacturers and sellers to distinguish their
products are claimed as trademarks. Where those designations appear in this book
and Adams Media was aware of a trademark claim, the designations have been
printed with initial capital letters.

The advice contained herein is for informational and entertainment purposes only.
Please consult your medical professional before beginning any exercise program,
your financial adviser before making investment decisions, and your nutritionist
before eating too many banana muffins. The author and publisher disclaim any
liability for any damage resulting from the use of the information contained in
this book.

*This book is available at quantity discounts for bulk purchases.
For information, please call 1-800-872-5627.*

To Scott, my reason why

SERENITY PRAYER FOR BAD BOY ADDICKTS

God grant me the serenity to dump the men I cannot change,
The courage to change the men I can,
And the wisdom to know the difference.

Contents

XIII   INTRODUCTION: SPOKEN LIKE A TRUE ADDICKT

1   CHAPTER 1
HOW DO YOU SPELL ADDICKTION?

15   CHAPTER 2
THE BAD, THE GOOD, AND THE GORGEOUS (THAT'S YOU)

STEP #1: Admit that you're vulnerable to rebellious natures and mischievous smiles—and that your dating habits have become downright unmanageable.

35   CHAPTER 3
MEET YOUR MATCH

STEP #2: Trust that there's a Power greater than La Perla that will return you to your center.

57 CHAPTER 4
GIVING IT UP

STEP #3: Make a conscious decision to hand your resolve and Friday nights over to the care of positive influences—even if that means spending QT with your little sister.

67 CHAPTER 5
I'M GOOD ENOUGH, I'M HOT ENOUGH . . .

STEP #4: Take a brave, probing look at your innermost smut—and admit to yourself, a Higher Power, and another person the juicy details of your honest mistakes.

81 CHAPTER 6
PLAYING NICE

STEP #5: You're absolutely, positively, bet-your-Louboutins-on-it convinced that you're ready to move past Addickt character flaws . . . and on to Nice Guy investments.

95 CHAPTER 7
WHAT DID YOU JUST CALL ME?

STEP #6: Humbly ask your Nice Guy to be patient with your limitations. This includes developing a relationship vernacular in which you won't confuse "I love you" with "Add me to your 401(k)."

107 CHAPTER 8

EMERGENCY ACTION

STEP #7: Forgive yourself if you cave. Applaud yourself if you don't. This is a process, girls. A process.

117 CHAPTER 9

EN-LIST YOUR GUILTY CONSCIENCE

STEP #8: Make a list of men, women, and supermodels you hurt as a Bad Boy Addickt and mentally prep to deal with every last one.

127 CHAPTER 10

REACH OUT AND TOUCH SOMEONE (BUT KEEP YOUR HANDS TO YOURSELF)

STEP #9: Make frank amends with those you hurt as a Bad Boy Addickt—unless doing so will damage them, others, or score you a restraining order.

139 CHAPTER 11

FROM YOUR MOUTH TO EVERYONE ELSE'S EARS

STEP #10: Continue to check in with your Addickt conscience—and when you screw up, don't be such an exhausting wimp. Admit it, already. . . .

147 **CHAPTER 12**
FAMILIAR TALES OF WHOA

STEP #11: Through meditation and support from the Addickt community, keep boosting your dating acumen. Couple your will with that of others to learn from their stories and mimic their careful and conscientious prowess.

159 **CHAPTER 13**
YOU'RE NOT SO BAD YOURSELF

STEP #12: Revel in your emotional, spiritual, and sexual awakening—and subtly spread the Bad Boy Addickt message to as many tartlets as you can.

169 **AFTERWORD: TAKE BACK THE NICE!**
173 **APPENDIX: HAVEN'T YOU HAD ENOUGH?**

Acknowledgments

ONCE AGAIN, SPECIAL THANKS to friends and family for their love and encouragement—especially Alia Malley, Allison Keane, Scott Mebus, Alva Polinsky, and Johnny Vulkan for their valuable input throughout. I'd also like to thank my editor, Jennifer Kushnier, and the entire staff at Polka Dot Press for their support. And finally, particular gratitude to my agent, Elisabeth Weed, for believing that Nice Guys really are the new black. And to think we settled for gray this long. . . .

Introduction

Spoken Like a True Addickt

FOR THE PAST TEN YEARS, I've played with a string of derelicts—one of whom, when I had bronchitis, considered smoking my last few American Spirits to be thoughtful first-aid. I've ridden on the backs of West Coast Choppers, canoodled with my married boss, and conditioned my olfactory senses to prefer men who reek of whiskey to those who dab on Acqua Di Parma. I've met Nice Guys before, but they often lack the laissez-faire attitude about life and love that I find unattainably delicious. It's the irresistible rogue who has the dizzying ability to drive women wild—with sexual abandon, with emotional frustration, with the will to submit, with the need to conquer. We rarely trust men who behave badly, yet we seldom stop ourselves from falling hard for their dishonest charm, unprincipled character, and fleeting attention. To date a sexy louse is to indulge a guilty pleasure—and very few women, myself included, would ever deny themselves the notorious drama of it all.

My name is Kristina . . . and I'm a Bad Boy Addickt.

The good news is that I'm not alone—and as someone who's reading this book for obvious reasons, neither are you. I can't tell you the number of women who confess to sharing a similar obsession with erratic charm and tousled bed head—but have no clue about how to alter their destructive dating patterns. Let me guess: In your heart, you want to adore a prince and know you deserve nothing less. But you also have no clue about how to transition from devouring one type to embracing another. You've worked hard at learning how to deal with and romanticize wayward trappings, dammit—and dating outside this world demands a serious psyche and paradigm shift. Would a sobering Nice Guy be a yawn in the bedroom? Would he smother you with attention—and would you lose your shit if he did?

Like most sensible women, I've always known I wouldn't spend forever with an attractively damaged man—but I never ceased to sneak one into my circle, falling harder and unfortunately becoming more hurt with each experience. So over three years ago, I decided to take responsibility for my actions. I could no longer rely on Bad Boys to falsely boost my self-confidence, hide tawdry dates from friends and family, or allow myself "just one more" at the end of a party. I was tired of the lies and apologies, all the more enabled by other women who became swept into the same uncontrollable cycle. So after a few centering chats with friends who'd also been there/done him, I made a conscious and determined decision to open myself up to The Other. I took a leap of faith, chased it with a strong cocktail—and before I knew it, fell madly in love with my very own Nice Guy.

However! The road to amour wasn't a seamless one, and it took months for me to recognize that "good" doesn't have to mean professionally boring, socially awkward, or emotionally wimpy. Good can often be the key to a wonderful relationship. Because this tattered-denim chaser was 1) able to recognize my problem and 2) ready to confront it, I developed my own

12-Step Program to dating recovery that's aimed at helping Bad Boy enthusiasts learn how to lead a fulfilling, randy, and rambunctious love life without an obvious jerk in tow. And you know what? It's reaped more benefits than wearing a crop top in a bar full of frat boys.

Don't get me wrong: I'm hardly a holier-than-thou success story, and by no means do I consider myself a "cured" case study. But that's actually the beauty of being a love life 12-Stepper. Because recovery isn't a quick fix but a committed process, you'll never earn the official title of "former" or "ex" (besides, you have enough of these prefixes already attached to your name). A sober love life is about knowing when to indulge your vices and when to control them. I know better than to forever swear-off Bad Boy bollocks or worry whether I'll be clean tomorrow. Instead, I concentrate on coping with naughty antics right now, one day at a time.

But enough about me! Without a doubt, this book will help all Bad Boy lovers realize that positive relationships with good-spirited men don't require sacrificing image, lowering standards, or changing social priorities for the dull at heart. To follow these 12 Steps is to work toward a satisfying, happy, and useful life—which, believe it or not, can exist without the wind in your hair or a hand down your pants.

Chapter 1

How Do You Spell Addicktion?

According to certified experts and paranoid mothers everywhere, addiction is typically characterized by a person's abnormal tolerance to and dependence on something that's psychologically, socially, or physically harmful and habit forming. When most people consider the term "addiction," they associate it with an inability to resist alcohol, donuts, shopping, sex, stalking, or heroin—and rightfully so. But that's not our concern here.

The problem we're dealing with is *addicktion*, not addiction—though I'm sure you can guess where there might be some overlap. Similar to its verbal inspiration, addicktion relates to an unhealthy obsession that takes one hell of a toll on your psyche. The crazy rush addickts experience after a one-night-stand and the morning-after headache of an emotional hangover aren't so unlike that which addicts undergo. In fact, addickts spiral into Bad Boy Benders, jones for quick hits, and have even been known to black out after one too many frisky encounters. You don't need William Safire to dissect the etymology of this word.

Though if you haven't guessed by now, the main differentiator between addiction and addicktion is that addicktion is about a woman's insatiable draw to, well, dicks. And by dicks, I'm talking about a man's personality, not his phallus—though when you're in deep, the two do tend to blur together. I won't go so far as to qualify addicktion as an illness, though you might want to check yourself for physical symptoms if you detect a highly compulsive need to surround yourself with innumerable creeps on a 24/7 basis.

So Where Do You Lay—Er, Stand?

To determine whether you're simply an addickt as defined by this 12-Step Program, start by running through the following list and checking off any qualities that describe you. This exercise might sound a bit too self-help for your sophisticated literary palate, but think of it as a way to determine just how much time you should devote to this book. I mean, if you're not as emotionally wasted as you thought, that's more time you can spend nuzzling in the shadows with a stranger, right?

Wrong! You're busted already. Now sharpen your #2, and don't make me do that again. You know you're an addickt when . . .

◆ You use Bad Boys to boost your self-confidence.
◆ You look forward to dimly lit occasions and think of them often.
◆ You try to control binges by changing the types of boys with whom you binge.
◆ You hide a man's boxer briefs, concert tees, or other left-behinds—and wear them in private.

- ◆ You sneak time with Bad Boys, and lie about your sneak to friends and family.
- ◆ You make friends with benefits at work (and we're not talking insurance plans).
- ◆ You choose not to remember the next day what was said or done the night before.
- ◆ You have morning sex to relieve severe guilt, fear, and emotional hangovers.
- ◆ You forget to eat or overeat during the throes of a Bad Boy chase.
- ◆ You make pledges never to indulge in another Bad Boy makeout session.
- ◆ You shake violently, hallucinate, or have convulsions to actually attract your next fling.

If you put a doodle next to at least three of the symptoms above, I'm afraid you may be a Bad Boy Addickt. The good news is that this blow is nothing compared to the time your deceitful ex said he believed in "don't ask/don't tell" relationships—and you were forced to play the role of an emotional deaf mute with a nice ass.

Talk about a reality check, eh? Contrary to stereotypical belief, a Bad Boy cannot be easily defined as, say, an unshaven man in a white T-shirt with a flip tendency to refer to your mother as "that smokin' hot chick . . . what's her name?" Real life doesn't send us such obvious signs—and one woman's neglectful date might be another's doting best friend, which is why it's unrealistic to define hard and fast Bad Boy "types" (more on this later). Universally, however, it's safe to say that Bad Boys misbehave. A selfish urge or momentary thrill navigates their lives—and each is well practiced at making their game an irresistible high.

Because a Bad Boy's qualities are behavioral symptoms and not carbon-copy prototypes, Bad Boys zoom in and out of our world in various clothes, classes, and cars. While one Bad Boy might invite you to sip port during sunset on Daddy's yacht, another could tackle you in the backseat of his Fiat and snort coke off your back.

Ultimately, what makes a Bad Boy such toxic dating material is how he specifically treats you—and soon causes you to doubt, squirm, cling, cry, overanalyze, and self-question. Your mood swings up one minute, and down the next. Not that you're quick to admit there's a problem. In fact, you're probably a pro at making excuses for a Bad Boy's dating tricks . . . just as you head back for more. In the next chapter, I'll list specific ingredients that make up the kind of Bad Boy elixirs that cause the evil spins. Until then, simply breeze through the next few paragraphs peppered with Bad Boy anecdotes and expect to nod your head in recognition. Neck cramps and a dewy forehead may be all you need to confirm that you've got a Bad Boy history on your hands.

 WARNING: Addickts spiral into Bad Boy Benders, jones for quick hits, and have even been known to black out after one too many frisky encounters.

Unlike most of your romances, once you acknowledge that you're an addickt, you won't feel isolated and alone. You'll have the support of recovered and recovering BBAs (that's insider talk for Bad Boy Addickts) who identify with and want to help women who walk in their stilettos. These sisters know how it feels to remove a Bad Boy's hand from the small of their backs, to turn walking hormones away from their doorstep, and to resist the urge to banter with a tawdry euphemism. After all, addicktion does not discriminate. It affects vulnerable women of all races, religions, and creeds. Addickts are your sister and your grandma, elementary school teachers and city bus drivers, supermodels and dental technicians, B-list actresses, self-help writers, and even senators from New York.

It's important to realize that you don't have to be a regular at the women's clinic or named the office slut to be an addickt. While extreme addickts have found themselves in hospitals, sanitariums, or jails—more in search of a little action, than as a result of their actions—you don't have to sink to such a severe low to be a love life 12-Stepper. You simply have to know that you deserve a man who won't screw you over, both for your own sake and those around you. (Your roommate only has so much sympathy left in her Pity Reserve for your "Why does this always happen to me?" stories.) Just think: Indulging in a 12-Step Program makes it all about you, for once. How refreshing is that?

Self-Respect, Naked Cheerios, and Paper Cuts

Quirky problem people are a tricky lot. I know, because I'm one of them. That's right: I'm a recovering BBA, too. And if you're like me, I'll bet you're almost a believer but still need a little convincing that you're more than just a restless young woman sowing her wild oats. But really, why so stubborn? Do I sense a bit of d-d-denial? All I know is that you didn't need to be cajoled into crashing the Young Republicans party with your liberal Italian stallion neighbor; and you definitely didn't have to be tied down to share a bowl of naked, morning-after Cheerios with your favorite rebound. And according to the checklist you completed earlier, it's obvious that you possess addickt qualities. So stick with me, here. Okay?

The next step is to test just how hard you really fall for deviant personalities. It may sound crazy at this stage, but I promise that once you realize how empowering it feels to align yourself with worthwhile male influences, you'll actually want to stay away from negligent cads. You know in the back of your head that the alternative to dating a great man is self-reproach, loneliness, despair, and a whole lot of rug burn. And when you look at your love life that way, you really have nothing to lose by admitting your BBA identity.

Now it's one thing to feel duped by a Bad Boy—and then pretend to ignore the effect he's had on you, which is often accomplished by subbing one tempting loser for another. But it's something different to actually see, on paper in front of you, just how much your head won't let you move on to cleaner sheets. Not to sound all Oprah, but you'll connect better with others once you connect with yourself. And you'll start to connect with yourself by taking the following quiz, which will help you kick your Bad Boy habits.

When it comes to your dating life, you've perfected the art of embracing the gray; but that's done shit for your sanity, so we're going to try a more black and white scale here. Answer "Um, Yeah . . . " or "Nope, Not Me" to the following questions to gauge how quickly you might want

"Right before meeting his parents for the first time, a boyfriend once said: 'Be yourself. Just . . . don't talk so much.' It took six years for him to become my EX-boyfriend." —Cara, 27

to toss your black book and dive into this one. Be honest, and don't beat yourself up if you answer "Um, Yeah . . . " to eight or more questions. Simply flip to Chapter 2 at breakneck speed—and don't you dare ask your ex to suck on those paper cuts.

1. Have you ever tried to date a new type of guy—only to find random fault with his neat hair, new sneakers, out-dated music, or geezer signature drink after just three dates (max)?
   ◇ Um, Yeah . . .
   ◇ Nope, Not Me

2. Do you wish friends and family would stop telling you who to date, no matter how much you complain about your crap track record—after incessantly bugging them for their advice?
   ◇ Um, Yeah . . .
   ◇ Nope, Not Me

3. Have you tried to swear off all men, in an effort to avoid making poor dating choices—you know, a boy-cott?
   ◇ Um, Yeah . . .
   ◇ Nope, Not Me

4. Have you ever called an easy-access ex, rebound, or fling for an ego boost when you've been crushed by a hot-n-heavy object de lust? Did you wait for him to arrive while curled in the fetal position with a heavy duvet pulled over your head?
   ◇ Um, Yeah . . .
   ◇ Nope, Not Me

5. Are you secretly jealous of friends who have relationships that balance intimacy with independence? That last longer than a few months? Whose exes don't grope another woman's hips in front of you, just days after you've broken up?

◇ Um, Yeah . . .
◇ Nope, Not Me

6. Have you ever called someone you're dating—only to then text, IM, e-mail, and call again if he doesn't contact you within, oh, three hours?

◇ Um, Yeah . . .
◇ Nope, Not Me

7. Have you ever saved a message, text, IM, or e-mail for 389 of your closest friends to meticulously analyze over, and over, and over . . . because he's so damn hard to read?

◇ Um, Yeah . . .
◇ Nope, Not Me

8. Are your most passionate encounters peppered with novelty, distance, and uncertainty?

◇ Um, Yeah . . .
◇ Nope, Not Me

9. Do you ever double-book yourself at night, just in case your date cancels at the last minute?

◇ Um, Yeah . . .
◇ Nope, Not Me

10. Do you ever accept a date up to one hour before you're tentatively supposed to meet—even though you thought (and hoped) he'd call sooner?

◇ Um, Yeah . . .
◇ Nope, Not Me

11. Do you tell yourself that you can stop dating slippery personalities any time you want, even though you keep dating them?

◇ Um, Yeah . . .
◇ Nope, Not Me

12. Have you ever missed classes, seminars, work, or personal training sessions because your head is spinning from the night before?

◇ Um, Yeah . . .
◇ Nope, Not Me

13. Have you ever called a friend at 5 A.M. after a wild night out, demanded she meet you for breakfast to debrief, cried, and sniffled on your way to the diner—and then sung the "Uh Oh" song by Lumidee until she threatened to plant your face in the sidewalk?

◇ Um, Yeah . . .
◇ Nope, Not Me

14. Do you ever try to get extra phone numbers at a party, because seven digits aren't enough?

◇ Um, Yeah . . .
◇ Nope, Not Me

15. Have you ever felt like your love life would be so much simpler if you lowered your standards?

◇ Um, Yeah . . .
◇ Nope, Not Me

16. Have you ever wondered why your "high" standards leave you feeling so low?

◇ Um, Yeah . . .
◇ Nope, Not Me

Because the Miami Sound Machine Can't Help You Now

How are you feeling? Pretty special, huh? Here's the thing: No matter how extreme your addicktion seems right about now, only you can decide if you're a BBA. Even if you swear on your ex's liver that you're not a three-letter girl, that you simply like to crawl out of your skin and into another's because you're the one in control, this choice is completely your call.

 WARNING: Contrary to stereotypical belief, a Bad Boy cannot be easily defined as, say, an unshaven man in a white T-shirt with a flip tendency to refer to your mother as "that smokin' hot chick . . . what's her name?"

I'm simply hoping that my 12 Steps will help you discover little gems about your dating patterns that might help tweak your priorities for the shiny better. As we go, I can't promise that you'll enjoy the tough love or familiar reflection staring back from the page. But I can vow that I'll never use the words "issues,"

"problems," or "Bad, bad, bad, bad boys/They make you feel so good!" to sway your thoughts one way or the other. (Gloria Estefan, by the way, married her first and only boyfriend. Enough said.)

If you haven't noticed by now, some of the logic behind *Addickted*'s 12-Step Program isn't too far off from AA's primary edicts. For example: If you don't have a first drink during recovery, then you can't have a tenth one. Similarly, if you don't have your way with a first Bad Boy, then you can't shag his ten friends—or something like that. I'm not about complete abstinence from all men, but I do endorse portion control. I know that the tempting ups of dating mischievous men include flattery, drama, spontaneity, complexity, sexual eccentricities, and erratic behavior—but with those highs, come the heinous downs of unreliability, moodiness, manipulation, shamelessness, irresponsibility, and erratic behavior. How such traits manifest themselves is little more than a grammar lesson about prepositional use, and not in a way that would thrill your fifth grade teacher. That is, a Bad Boy exhibits these qualities to you, about you, in you, over you, through you, around you—not to mention, above you and under you. But that last part goes without saying.

Although our ultimate goal is for you to feel comfortable getting mushy with a Nice Guy, that doesn't mean you must completely banish Bad Boys from your orbit. I'd never suggest you quarantine yourself to a padded room with "Hang in there!" kitty posters and a copy of *Buddhism for Dummies*. Instead, learn to re-appropriate a Bad Boy's purpose, and take advantage of his skills outside a candlelit restaurant (think: handyman, creative consultant . . .). This way, risky men won't completely exit your life, but simply hang out on the safe but valued periphery. Let's face it: If Bad Boys were monsters at heart, you wouldn't fall for them in the first place. It's just that they often make better friends or associates than they do partners d'amour. What's most important is that you'll emerge from this 12-Step experience as an evolved, insightful woman—with yet another complicated and overanalyzed love lesson tucked under your belt for personal growth and juicy storytelling. Only this time, your tale will have a happy ending.

Chapter 2

The Bad, the Good, and the Gorgeous (That's You)

STEP #1: Admit that you're vulnerable to rebellious natures and mischievous smiles—and that your dating habits have become downright unmanageable.

Every girl has a story about her first time. And then she has a story about her first time with a Bad Boy. Mine began with feverish e-mail foreplay, led to an inexplicable need to lick his crooked bottom tooth, and climaxed during our first casual date, which involved dodgy wine and his even dodgier female friend—who happened to bear a striking resemblance to a squirmy little rat, but I digress.

Though I didn't recognize it under the influence of dim lights and an open bar, my first time spotlighted many of the key, universal elements that draw nice women to naughty men. Said Bad Boy knew how to tease with humor, tempt with imperfections, and feed curiosity with questionable drinks and unexpected company. He sealed the deal with a kiss and phone number swap, all at a fast and furious pace. By the time I crawled into bed that night, my cell phone rang and the voice on the other end wanted to know if I'd gotten home safely—and if we could have dinner the next evening. Though my mind was thinking, "What the hell just happened? Don't go—this boy is trouble . . ." my mouth couldn't say the words "I'd love to!" quickly enough.

We lasted four bumpy months before I learned in an utterly dramatic way (Friends barged in on our date! Drinks were thrown in faces! Tears were shed in the bathroom!) that when he wasn't spending marathon weekends with me, he clocked weekdays with the rodent from our first encounter. The whole thing's such a predictable yawn in retrospect that I don't even expect you to gasp. Yet the push, the pull, the cinematic pace of it all—the process broke my heart, but managed to rope me in for more, more, more! Not with this dolt, of course; but with variations on his theme. Call me an extremist, but before this first Bad Boy stumbled into my line of vision, I dated a very nice, very safe publishing executive who studied art history and quoted *The New Yorker*. If we didn't pass Sunday afternoons antiquing, we spent nights drinking expensive bottles of wine in Central Park—properly concealed in a container from the Museum of Modern Art (for legal and aesthetic purposes, you see).

Our three years together were lovely. Love-ly! But when our relationship came to a very ho-hum end, I couldn't wait to wrap my arms and legs around the unexpected deviant. No wonder my first fling with a Bad Boy was so irresistible. In art and in love, contrast alone can be a very powerful force.

Naughty Boys Need Love Too?

Those who've done time with Bad Boys know just how easy it is to find their hearts, minds, and bodies at the mercy of an unruly personality. We tell ourselves that Bad Boys can be tamed by the right woman; that their conflicted souls require special forgiveness; that we really are the only woman for whom they shout their feelings from fire escapes at midnight. And we convince ourselves of these unwavering truths, no matter how much a little voice in our heads (not to mention, pretty loud ones from friends) insists we're kidding ourselves.

Here's what you secretly know but hate to hear: Bad Boys wield their power because we allow them to—partially, because we keep coming back for more. Bad Boys are like special French panties that come apart in the wash: No matter how carefully we fold them into a lingerie sack to avoid snagging or buy gentle detergent to massage their fragile fabric, it takes only one loose thread for the whole mess to unravel. Does this stop us from replacing our lacy lovelies with a new pair, exactly like the old? Of course not. We simply tell ourselves that it was our fault they fell apart, or that they had a unique defect, or that the next pair will be different . . . when the plain truth is: Sometimes overpriced underwear isn't what it's cut out to be.

 WARNING: Bad Boys wield their power because we allow them to—partially, because we keep coming back for more.

The primary link between disappointing undies and disappointing men is the perception—by them and by us—that they're somehow so damn special. To yield a little insight into the Bad Boy brain, I have a friend named Bennett who's quite a rascal. His mantra for every dalliance and emotional misstep is—and I quote—"special rules for special people." Unless we're talking about my Uncle Carl and his scoot-about, I personally find this a hard sell in any play-nice-with-others department.

But Bennett is tall and angular, with Mediterranean good looks. In a word, he's edible. He boasts a sculpted nose and olive-toned skin, while his eyes remind me of Benicio Del Toro's. They're piercing, with a devilish glint and unexpectedly attractive bags that whisper "experience" rather than "old man, get a tuck." On lonely nights I've imagined rolling myself up in the folds of skin under his baby blues, and pulling them tight to my chin as one would a security blanket.

And that's part of a Bad Boy's charm, too: Bennett and his cohorts are acutely aware of just how and when to give women what they need. If you crave quiet and solace, as I often did after a long day, a Bad Boy will create a soothing environment (steak au poivre at a dimly lit bistro). If you need to escape, check your mailbox for tickets to Miami (and the promise of a king size bed). A Bad Boy will read you, take you, and lick fudge off your belly until the sun rises and sets on your naked bodies. In a Bad Boy's mind, there are no victims—just volunteers. And to an extent, he's right. When a Bad Boy trades responsible behavior for your pleasure, it's easy to become a believer—in your personal value and his selflessness and perceived devotion.

The interesting thing is, Bennett didn't always treat his dates as arm-dazzling throwaways. He used to be a Committed Man, who didn't believe that one chap could have the power to take advantage of so many women's vulnerabilities for his own benefit. Bennett's priorities changed, though, when an opportunistic roommate *told* him it was possible—and Bennett's personal experiences supported the theory. As Bad Boy legend has it, Bennett was a college freshman angling to break up with his old girlfriend before moving onto the next. That's when said roommate assured him he could realistically juggle both. The plan? He'd work one woman into his schedule for family holidays and a weekly dinner, and book the other for steamy nights on the town. Bennett questioned whether he could pull off the Casanova act, but he quickly found success and a brand new identity. The two women in his life let Bennett coast like a bike without brakes for one whole year. That's a lot of face-sucking in boy time.

Ever since, Bennett's diligently perfected an MO that makes every girl on his social calendar feel like she's The One. Why? Because 1) he's attractive; 2) he thinks he's special; and 3) women let him. It's really that simple. And just to confirm Bennett's credibility, dear readers: He usually rotates four women at once, while holding down a steady girlfriend—you know, on average.

Now before you lose all hope in dating humanity, remember that Bennett is no different than the lace panties we spoke of earlier: beautiful and damaged, yes. But he's also easily replaceable. In the next few chapters, you'll learn how to shop for a new type of man who doesn't require a special cycle to keep your romance intact—and yet feels all too perfect against your bare skin.

Bennett, Bennett . . . Wherefore Art Thou Bennett?

Because I care more about helping you than ruining Bennett's game, I feel the need to relay the inside scoop that he's told me—on rare, vulnerable, drunken occasions—about the way a Bad Boy's mind works. Though you may never date Bennett himself, you've likely fallen for a Bennett multiple times. Straight from the Bad Boy's mouth, here's what Bennett has to say about his own kind.

Mr. B insists that Bad Boys are the biggest romantics you'll ever meet. Sounds perfect, right? They will wine you, dine you, they'll book a one-way trip to Nassau on the dreamy off-chance that you'll never return. In short, a Bad Boy will promise you the

world on a parsley-garnished plate . . . or the back
of his Vespa, depending on his style. The problem
is that he'll do all of these things as much for his
own ego as he will for your pleasure—in an effort
to learn whether you fit his narrowly defined view
of perfection, should he ever decide to integrate
perfection into his life.

As Bennett puts it, not all romantics believe in
love; some simply believe in romance. If they're
spoiled enough, they might even think love is
overrated—which, if you think about it, is more
than a bit backward. A romantic who thinks
love is overrated? That's like a yoga teacher who
hates to stretch or a Jew for Jesus. But according
to Bennett, romance is simply a means to having
a good time.

So what? you're thinking. *I like to have fun too!*
But here's the mind muddle: In most women's
heads and hearts, having fun is a means to falling in love. We can't help ourselves. One is a
superhighway that leads to the other, and most
of the time we run red lights to get there without
stopping to pay tolls. But in a Bad Boy's head,
having fun is often a means to . . . having more
fun. This leads to lavish dinners, frequent sex,
wild adventures, great anecdotes—and most
importantly, a very captive audience (you).

Not that he sticks around for long. As Bennett once asked a woman in a poorly timed, post-
coital moment, "Why can't I just love women in
general? Why do I have to pick and commit to

"A guy I hooked up with called me the wrong name in the morning. I didn't correct him, and then hooked up with him again the next night."—Alison, 21

one and only one?" The man assures me that he means every compliment he tells a woman . . . at that moment. And that he's been in love . . . in his own way. Not that this means jack for his dates in the long run, but do note Bennett's afterthoughts, ladies: Special rules for special people. . . .

Personally, I think *you're* too special for that.

So Do Bad Boys Ever Commit?

Naturally, there are more than a few reformed Bad Boys who've learned to appreciate monogamy of any sort. But according to Bennett, most only marry for three reasons: 1) *I'm getting older.* 2) *I'm getting fatter.* 3) *I'm getting balder.* So unless you're into aging, blubbery, and hairless losers, I hope you're starting to realize that it's time to graze in nicer pastures. Everyone has an expiration date, but the only thing more pathetic than a washed-up Bad Boy is a desperate, washed-up Bad Boy in elastic-waist pants toting a pillbox of Viagra. Is this the kind of man you've been praying would come around? I think not.

Why Bad Men Are Like Rotten Melons

Sniffing out a Bad Boy isn't so different from detecting a bad melon: a sour smell, unhealthy coloring, and a few shakes for loose seeds can save you a whole lot of heartburn. But this requires physically handling a man, and our goal is to stop the need to lay a manicured finger on him long before your compulsion kicks in. The tricky thing is, all melons look alike for the most part—and not all Bad Boys do. I wish I could simply suggest you steer clear of men in tattoos, rumpled blazers, and creative facial hair, but the way a Bad Boy looks is often such a small part of his appeal. In fact, one woman's Monster Truck driver in Illinois looks nothing like another's Brit Rock transplant in Los Angeles—though they both may share similar Bad Boy traits. So we'll skip the obvious physicality and cut to the Character Cocktail that makes Bad Boys feel so universally right at a tenuous moment—yet prove to be oh so wrong for a life that lasts longer than a seriously hot kiss.

You've already identified that you have a problem, which we know from far too many public service announcement spoofs is the first step to admitting you're in trouble. But because you are an addickt, you may find the next few paragraphs a bit challenging—not because I malign your taste, insist you're a lost cause, ask you to dig into your past, or complete another self-evaluation quiz. The next few paragraphs will make you break one mean sweat because I'm going to dissect more than a few delicious details about Bad Boys, so don't be surprised when your hormones do back flips as we go. Hell, I might even need to take a cold shower after I type them. But there's a well-intentioned method to my madness. In fact, there are a few.

First, it's important to note that Bad Boys are not special, that their archetypal appeal is widespread and even quite unoriginal. This may come as a surprise, but they're actually more alike than the Nice Guys you avoid. In Bad Boys' quests to be uniquely hip, smooth, and irresistible, they simply tend to ditto each other's behavior. The minute you recognize a series of familiar qualities in different men, over and over again, my money's on a serious gag reflex.

Second, it's necessary to specifically itemize a Bad Boy's qualities so you can better recognize a Nice Guy's attributes when you experience them—if just by contrast. You know how you can become absolutely enraptured with one man? But once he's history, the way he laughs or sniffs or eats really fast while holding his fork like a shovel becomes just plain annoy-ing? Especially when you compare him to the men you've met since? Well, I'll bet that really reading, and then internalizing, a Bad Boy's qualities will give you that "over it" feeling the next time you meet someone Nice. To know where one man's appeal ends is to see where the other's begins. A Bad Boy cannot exist without a Nice Guy to complement him.

Finally, I want you to pay close attention to these Bad Boy personas, because I want you to want them in your life one last time. No really, I do. I want you to crave their touch, their smell, and their taste so badly that you're tempted to speed dial not one, but three booty calls—just so your backups have backups. I want you to want this, not because I'm a sadistic bitch or in self-righteous recovery, but because I want you to be reminded as you move down the list, licking your lip gloss and planning your next conquest, just how unmanageable your dating pat-terns have become. I want you to remember this anxious need because it's exactly this feeling that you'll be fighting against for the next 11 Steps. And you will only get better from here.

The Character Cocktail*

For the purpose of beating your addicktion, I'd like to pres-ent an unofficial list of traits that define a Bad Boy. I've dubbed it the Character Cocktail, simply because every Bad Boy's

---

*You do realize there's no way I could itemize every last Bad Boy descriptive because a scoundrel's psycho-graphics could go on and on for pages—and even I don't have the stomach for that. Plus, as I mentioned earlier, what defines a Bad Boy is how he makes a woman feel, rather than what he specifically is or does. The point here is to recognize, nauseate, and move on.

disposition includes a generous mix of at least three ingredients listed below—and indulging in one too many can make a girl sick to her stomach.

○ Dismissive enough to make you want him more

○ Accessible enough to make you think you can have it

○ Mysterious

○ A study in contradictions

○ Refreshingly candid

○ Startlingly unapologetic

○ Disregards boundaries

○ Dishonest

○ Mischievous

○ Coercively argumentative and defiant

○ Endearingly acquiescent

○ Emotionally damaged by clinical standards (think: depressed, angry, or obsessive)

○ Excessively flattering

○ Has a short attention span

○ Self-involved

○ Exhibits extreme emotions or actions

○ Selfish yet introspective

(continued)

○ Drinks or self-medicates more than he should

○ Initiates drama

○ Snubs everyone but you

○ Sexually forward

○ Hypocritical

○ Adventurous

○ Feigns virtue

○ Has questionable intentions

○ Has unquestionable charm

○ Risk-taker

○ Unlimited charisma

○ Loves a good double entendre

○ Unfaithful

○ Expects you to fit within his idealistic, narrowly defined vision of "how it's supposed to be"

○ Changes his definition of The Ideal Woman, once he realizes you might fit his paradigm

Now the only thing worse than confronting the fact that your dating history is full of double-fisting Bad Boy cocktails, is recognizing how much effort you've put into justifying your past. Obviously, you're not the first addickt to long for comfort zones with men who recoil from them—especially when a Bad Boy possesses personality snafus that trick you into thinking he's something he's not. For instance, a Bad Boy's clingy need for validation can be mistaken for undivided attention. Unbridled passion may be compensation for crap conversational skills. A wandering eye might be interpreted as people watching. . . .

When you're clocking hours with a Bad Boy, it's not unusual to tell yourself that emotional bruises are simply "learning experiences"—or that your Bad Boy track record is the result of bad karma. After all, you've trained yourself to swallow panic like pills without water: Your Bad Boy does work late. Gulp. You do tend to over-scrutinize missed phone calls and delayed text messages. Gulp. Gulp. And didn't your horoscope say something about misaligned planets? Gulp. Gulp. Gulp. You tell yourself that fate will take care of you. That there are no heroes or villains, just people with unfortunate pasts and well-intentioned souls. That the trick to finding the right guy, is to land someone whose quirks and faults play off your own—a crooked yin to your off-kilter yang, so to speak. That until you meet The One, with his vintage T-shirt collection and intuitive compassion, you'll conquer Bad Boy frustrations by taking the high road or playing aloof. Hey, at least you'll have wild stories to tell your grandkids. If you're really ambitious, maybe even a bestselling memoir. You're not settling, you tell yourself. You're living. . . .

As a BBA, I always found that no matter how many times I told myself those things, one detail always threw me: I swore that I understood, *I mean really empathized*, with the whys behind every Bad Boy's disposition—and without the slightest sign of judgment. I never wanted them to change, but I did hope they'd change because of me. Yet in the end, not one word, thought, or deed ever mattered. Forget delusions of grandeur, babe. As a BBA, I'd entered denial territory. An addickt might as well be crowned Queen Hypothetical, one who allows the What-If Games to run amuck in her otherwise clever little head. Of course, denial for me was an exercise in self-preservation. I've even been known to let internal dialogues take on lives of their own. I'll bet you can relate.

If he doesn't call, you think:
"What if his cell's stuck between the seats of his Budget rental car that's now parked in Nevada?"

If he stands you up, you think:
"What if he's working late instead of shagging his leggy supervisor in the executive bathroom?"

If he disappears altogether, you think:
"What if he's dead?"

So Are All Bad Boys Alike?

Of course not. If I could draft a list of stereotypical Bad Boy prototypes—from jobs, to friends, to social agendas, to past relationship cues—I would. But the more addickts I spoke with, the more I realized that everyone defines a Bad Boy differently because their allure and frustrations are more behavior-driven than demographically defined. When it comes to work, for example, some Bad Boys are highly devoted to their graphic design jobs—while others drive UPS trucks and picket the union. What I have learned from my own experience is that you can spot (and later avoid) a Bad Boy by projecting how his attitude will affect your feelings, according to the Character Cocktail I noted earlier. This takes a great deal of self-awareness, not to mention self-control. By the book's end, you'll have mastered both.

I will say this, however: A Bad Boy's relationship with his friends often mimics the way he treats his girlfriends. Most Bad Boys have an extended network of friends, but plow through them easily. The turnaround time on relationships, friend or otherwise, can be whiplash fast because a Bad Boy's personality spews charisma and unreliability. Their careless, reckless devotion and lack of sensitivity do not a long-term BFF make. They've mastered the casual and often generous funship, but are still a bit clueless about how to maintain a devoted, long-term friendship. When pals do stick around, they're likely to be women who are more forgiving and nurturing by nature. (No, you're not being neurotic. These chicks probably are past conquests, too.)

When they're out on the town, Bad Boys are game for all things novel and curious—due to an insatiable need to exploit a potentially risky situation. Sometimes this includes dating sweet you, because your intentions are pure enough. To some extent, it's even validating for a Bad Boy to couple himself with a Nice Girl if only to prove to himself that he's not completely insane. If he's the type of Bad Boy in need of rescue, he likely reasons that someone else's good heart will do the dirty work for him—which is where your Need to Be Needed side comes in.

"My ex-husband had a post office box while we were married where he received letters from a former girlfriend. I still wonder just how 'former' she really was...."
—Caroline, 34

Too Much Drama:
Celebrity Good Boys Gone Bad

Tinsel Town has historically churned out infamous Bad Boys—and for years, we liked it that way. But lately, there seems to be a disturbing trend among the sweeter set to intentionally trade in their moral charm for that of the classic wanker. Have the more pleasant celebrity elite been blinded by flashing paparazzi bulbs or the shine off their new Hummer? Too many Nice Guys have gone to the Dark Side—and aren't coming back anytime soon. The thing is, they tend to look like a clumsy gang of poseurs, and nobody likes an oversaturated market of phonies. Personally, I suspect they'll subtract from Bad Boy cachet and make the whole lot look lame. Here, a few "Bad Boys" (quotes intentional) I can only expect will ruin it for their mentors.

LANCE ARMSTRONG: I'm thrilled he beat cancer, I really am. But did he need to thank his wife for her loyalty by serving her with divorce papers and running off with a lithe rock star? And that didn't even last.

BILL CLINTON: Questioned, and eventually refused to commit to, a concrete definition of sex—and duped the United States into following his lead. Need I say more?

BILLY CRUDUP: Left his wife for another woman, when the former was pregnant with his child. The first part of his last name says it all.

CARSON DALY: Fell into the arms of virgin Jennifer Love Hewitt, and then between the legs of party girl Tara Reid.

HARRISON FORD: I'm not sure what's worse: Divorcing your wife, dating an emaciated starlet, or piercing your ear ten years after it's no longer hip. Talk about a midlife crisis Bad Boy. . . .

JOSH HARTNETT: What happened to his high school sweetheart? Oh, right. He dumped her to work the celebrity circuit, pelvis first.

ETHAN HAWKE: Fell for a barely legal model on set, with a beautiful wife and charming kids at home. Saved by karma, Uma now glows and Ethan eats crow. The man's never looked so gnarly.

BRAD PITT: Traded in the pretty girl next door for a siren with lips like an air mattress. Two divorces, a penchant for accessorizing with vials of blood, and a need to swap spit with her brother obviously evoke a certain je ne sais quoi. Don't you agree?

But as you've learned, it's hard to control what was never really manageable in the first place.

Reel Life Versus Real Life: The Hollywood Ending

I'd like to thank the Academy for encouraging addickts to believe in Hollywood endings. It's not your fault that you have a hard time knowing when to shut off your sparkling imagination. On the silver screen, the female lead almost always lands, dupes, tames, or outwits the Bad Boy to her benefit—that is, if he doesn't come around on his own. We've seen this plot emerge in classic films like *Pride and Prejudice* and dating flicks like *Reality Bites* and *Singles*. How can such a popular theme *not* warm our precious little cockles? What's more, all women tend to translate actors' Hollywood personas to their real-life characters; voyeuristic tabloid reports and reality TV, which are the tastiest of guilty pleasures, help us piece together their otherwise mysterious lives. On and off the clock, celebrity Bad Boys seem to play on the erotic edge of danger—and I'll admit that it can be downright irresistible. To an extent. . . .

Let's spin through the standard It List of Hollywood Honeys who make us simultaneously swoon and shudder—if for no other reason than to prove how futile our salivating can be. Who can resist Hugh Grant's fluttering eyelids and self-deprecating humor? His Bad Boy status was confirmed when he banged Divine Brown while dating Elizabeth Hurley (if that's not self-destructive, I don't know what is). Each time George Clooney, the untouchable bachelor, says he'll never get married, one more woman decides she'll be the one to change his mind. Jeremy Piven's dismissive yet razor-sharp wit fuels fantasies about silencing his attitude with a serious smooch. And no matter how many pounds he gains or telephones he chucks, Russell Crowe's mischievous eyes call addickts back for more. Of course, few Bad Boys could ever be outdone by Jude Law: When this deceptive bloke cheated on his beautiful fiancée, his exploits encouraged women to drop out of med school with the hope of becoming a bottle-blonde nanny. Oh, the diaries they could sell to *US Weekly*!

 WARNING: It's not unusual to tell yourself that emotional bruises are simply "learning experiences" or that your Bad Boy track record is the result of bad karma.

No wonder addickts revel in notorious Bad Boys who drip love, sex, and heartache from their very core—even if we're smart enough to know that off-screen, their roles are also scripted by publicists. (For example, media insiders gossip that Colin Farrell's an angel. Who knew?) Yet the dark, cool, edgy, dirty details of a Bad Boy's life and work ignite an addickt's imagination when the two mix and mingle. In both scenarios, we watch their victims play with fire and come out on top— often, quite literally. The problem is, women reappear in the spotlight unscathed and dressed in Dior. Let's face it: Hollywood Bad Boys are attractive train wrecks who most of us will never meet. For an addickt, the next best thing to star-studded drama is to stalk their doppelgangers in the office lunchroom or at the local watering hole.

Does all this talk of wrangling a Hollywood hunk sound tempting? Discouraging? Don't dwell. There are the rare, genuine occasions when celebrity Bad Boys actually turn adorably good. Case in point: Johnny Depp. The chain-smoking, tattoo-laden specimen has the looks of a heartthrob but refuses to play one on the big screen. For years, he dated shoplifters and drug addicts—all while shunning the Hollywood studio system. Hell, he even shunned his own country! Now, Monsieur Depp has taken up with a French beauty and committed to raising their children in a stable relationship across the pond. As ideal as this union sounds, don't overthink it. The man's already taken. And as much as you buy into Hollywood whimsies, you have to admit that overindulgence is one slick hair short of fan club membership—and you outgrew signed posters in seventh grade.

Chapter 3

Meet Your Match

STEP #2: Trust that there's a Power greater than La Perla that will return you to your center.

During recovery, it's important to seek refuge in a trusted source that's previously brought you inner solace. Whether this is a church, a park, a therapist's office, or the Nars cosmetic counter at Saks is up to you. What's important here is that you discover a Higher Power that exists within these havens—and, depending on how spiritual you are, exists within yourself.

Hiding under a Bad Boy's arm might be a familiar scenario, and though familiar feels good, this doesn't mean it will help you feel settled. Much like a push-up bra, Bad Boys are a quick fix to an otherwise droopy situation. Addicktion is often symptomatic of a bigger problem, need, or lack of fulfillment. Perhaps you have commitment hesitations that stem from family problems or difficulty with authority figures; trust issues that are caused by possessive exes; self-doubt that stems back to high school clique alienation.

Whatever your concern, addicktion often manifests itself as the obvious clue to a larger personal debacle. As you move through each forthcoming chapter and exercise, take the time to probe deeper about why you've always attached yourself to so many Bad Boys in the first place. If it hasn't been a lifelong habit, find the trigger point that set your moxie in motion— and slowly but surely, analyze its impact with your Higher Power. You'll be surprised at how connected your addicktion may be to stumbling blocks that exist outside the confines of your love life.

As you gradually place your belief in a strengthening source, your scope will begin to expand beyond your obvious social outlets (Bad Boys) and into less expected realms of comfort (Nice Guys). Personally, I'm so tired of hearing great women whine, *Where are all the good guys hiding?* Once and for all, girls: They're not! Nice Guys are the least likely to conceal their whereabouts—though BBAs are probably too preoccupied with a mysterious, corner-lurking rogue to notice. The minute you realize there's a Power greater than your wicked libido and coy wiles to excite you and the company you keep, you'll begin to attract Nice Guys—which actually saves you time actively looking for them. Nice Guys aren't impressed with the super-ficialities you use to reel in Bad Boys. They're more impressed with who you are than what you can do for them.

Giving in to this side of your true identity will take some reading, self-reflection, and meditation. Hey, I never said it wasn't work. But as you hone the talents and interests that define who you are, Nice Guys will gravitate to your inner glow because you're shedding a previously sketchy skin that no longer serves its purpose. In fact, you'll bump into Nice Guys on your journey because you're starting to explore new activities that invite new company. And unless these activities include assisting photographer Terry Richardson or joining a Brett Easton Ellis fan club, you're probably safe from inundat-ing yourself with Emotional Mishaps.

As you slowly and inevitably integrate Nice Guys into your world, for the love of heavy petting, please be sure to do so on a platonic level. Because I'd never expect you to go cold turkey from all men, feel free to consider Nice Guys the nicotine gum or nonalcoholic beer of dating addicktion. Look around, hot stuff: Chances are, a lot of your close male friends are either 1) Nice Guys or 2) men who walk a safe line between Bad and Nice. Beating your addicktion is about changing your lifestyle. Thus, introducing Nice Guys into your world as friends, confidants, or support systems is a must. You'll not only grow from their unconditional generosity, but subconsciously appreciate them as part of a larger Nice Guy collective. This way, when you're actually ready to date a Nice Guy, the jump won't feel like such a giant leap of faith.

Bring on the Nice Guy . . .

Though Bad Boys will receive plenty of airtime throughout this book, let's transition to the sobering Nice Guy demo before you forget how miserable it is to fall for men who love themselves more than they love you. Though you're nowhere near ready to date a Nice Guy, I want to plug their best attributes into your memory now, so that you have a strong basis of comparison and very real impetus to work hard at kicking that Bad Boy habit. Plus, you should know a few details about what your love life will be like—and become intimately familiar with Nice Guys' ups, downs, ins, and outs so that you can mentally prep for the transition.

Remember how I mentioned that in most women's minds, having fun is a means to falling in love, but in Bad Boys' minds, having fun is simply a means to having more fun? Well, with Nice Guys, having a good time is actually (brace yourself, BBA) a means to having more fun *and* falling in love. I realize this sounds like a no-brainer, but we all know the brain isn't exactly our most active organ when we're in the initial stages of dating . . . at least not as a BBA.

 WARNING: Nice Guys only *seem* to move faster than Bad Boys because their intentions are more sincere than what you're used to experiencing.

First things first though: I need you to quell your nervous suspicion that Nice Guys will be clingier than cellophane and ready to commit before you are. Contrary to popular belief, Nice Guys only *seem* to move faster than Bad Boys because their intentions are more sincere than what you're used to experiencing. Mark my words: A Bad Boy will tell you who he is within the window of your first three dates. He'll come on strong and anxious for your approval, spill private stories that yield the impression he trusts you, talk about dating successes and failures—and frost his diatribe with a thick layer of compliments. Bad Boys know how to manipulate a woman's emotions. They're experts at balancing self-deprecation and honesty with just enough flattery to convince you that you're easy to talk to *and* fabulous to look at. But does all this make for a winning combo? Not exactly.

I don't know about you, but I always assumed that a person who's willing to confide in me about his father's jail time or how many antidepressants he pops a day might be in it for the long haul. Sadly, that's not the case. What I did eventually learn from these tête-à-têtes was not that most Bad Boys are introspective and in search of conversational soul mates—but that I had to force myself to actively listen to the very obvious info they threw my way. Once, I went on a date with a man who hid his Bad Boy-isms under a very delightful exterior: He ran his family business, was adored by elderly neighbors, and even went to church. But on our first date—somewhere between "Do you have any siblings?" and "Please pass the ketchup"—this slick Bad Boy managed to slip in the words: "You do know I don't do commitments." My reply? "And I just published a book on dumping men. I think you've met your match." I assumed he wanted to banter; after all, who'd say such a thing on a first date?! Cut to four months later: The Bad Boy and I were at a concert when he delivered the familiar words, "Kristina, you do know I don't do commitments . . ."—only this time he wanted to break up. If I'd been more intent on hearing this guy's warning rather than impressing him with witticisms, I would have walked out before our first dessert.

In my case and others I've been told about, it's not that addickts don't care when Bad Boys say they recoil at commitments or that they're already seeing other people—and by the way, one just happens to be hiding in the powder room as we speak. It's that a Bad Boy's magnetism is so damn convincing that we're positive he'll fall in love against his initial instincts because he created these self-defined provisions before he even met us. To be fair, some Bad Boys do eventually convert to the Nice Guy lifestyle. But in many cases, they simply like to play. And if you're an addickt, the overused word "player" is all we need to say to define your type, because I'm sure you've put your dating habits on repeat—and they're now beyond your control.

The good news is that if you let a Nice Guy work his magic, there will be no subtext to his compliments, dinner invites, or makeout sessions. He'll sincerely use traditional dating tactics to—wait for it—get to know you better. Of course, just because he's a Nice Guy doesn't mean he's an easy catch. His words, thoughts, and actions may come more quickly and with more sincerity, but a Nice Guy once told me that when moving forward in a relationship, his intentions have been known to get lost in translation. Here's how: While most women won't accept a date with a man unless he nails the criteria on her Dreamy Boyfriend Checklist (is he funny? successful? family-oriented?), a Nice Guy will ask a woman out, and then continue to date her—until he collects enough proof of their compatibility to decide that he's smitten.

My point: Just because you've enjoyed four dinners in one week with a Nice Guy does not mean he's more into you than he is. He likes what he knows, but needs to know more. So take a deep breath because when you're together, you don't have to worry about whether a Nice Guy will want to rush a relationship or need too much from you, too soon. He can be a feisty challenge—if not more so than a Bad Boy, because this new one's dating formula is unfamiliar. How convenient, then, that addickts are such big fans of unpredictability and defiant imperfections.

What a Yummy Surprise!

As your Higher Power and growing sense of self gradually work their magic, you'll begin to recognize that the Nice Guys in your life are more complex than you ever realized. As much as I'd love to chop all men into two neat little categories of Good and Bad, you and I both know that there's going to be some overlap. And with this news comes the scrumptious truth that your future Nice Guy might be someone else's current Bad Boy. That's right. You don't need me to tell you that people evolve and situations provoke. Because men aren't one-dimensional, various stimulae and personalities create perceptions of Good and Bad that unveil themselves in different ways to different women. So once you're ready to start dating again, don't try to spot a Nice Guy by simply looking for a cuffed hem or comparing yourself to the Pollyannas he bedded before you. Besides, beating an addicktion has less to do with the guy himself and more to do with how his personality, lifestyle, and sensibilities affect you. You can't judge a Bad Boy or Nice Guy by his style, job, or interests. His ID stems more from how he treats you than anything else.

Obviously, your ultimate goal is to break that rotten dating run and reap the benefits of a healthy dynamic. But that doesn't mean dating a Nice Guy is the easy answer to pain-free singlehood; better yet, consider it an alternative lifestyle that will open you up to new men and smarter choices. Just as I listed key ingredients in the Character Cocktail of a Bad Boy, I'm going to do the same with those of a Nice Guy—except call this one a Spirit Smoothie. Similar to your favorite post–spin class banana, strawberry, and flaxseed concoction, a Nice Guy will be a healthy and refreshing change from the Character Cocktails that wreak havoc on your dating constitution.

The Spirit Smoothie*

Think of a Nice Guy as a nutritious smoothie that feeds your spirit and satisfies your cravings for some seriously good lovin'. Note how perfectly these Nice Guy qualities blend together to create a delicious whole—whether you occasionally chug one as a supplement during recovery or eventually add them to your diet on a regular basis. If a Nice Guy's Smoothie-worthy, he'll boast at least six of the sweet ingredients below. Drink up!

○ Charitable

○ Forgiving

○ Empathetic

○ Respectful

○ Communicative

○ Happy to compromise

○ Selectively strong-willed

○ Sexually unpredictable

○ Value-driven   (continued)

---

*As with the Character Cocktail, Smoothie ingredients include, but are not limited to, a Nice Guy's most outstanding traits. I could go on about how a Nice Guy is generous, attentive, and mentally stable—but only you know the personality mix that makes your belly all warm and fuzzy. Plus, let's face it: You already know a Nice Guy's best talking points if you think hard enough. They're the qualities you adore in your girlfriend, brother, dog, or doorman; basically, the attributes that make you feel special, happy, safe, supported, and loved.

○ Treats your family and friends as his own

○ Makes a conscious effort to fit into your world

○ Surprises you with thoughtful treats

○ Modest

○ Understands timing

○ Complimentary

○ Genuine

○ Knows when to put you on a pedestal—and when to take you down

○ Calms your fears, neuroses, and stress levels

○ Balances your shortcomings

○ Patient

○ Protective

○ Supportive

○ Consistent

○ Apologetic

○ Honest

○ Altruistic

○ Harmless intentions

○ Appreciative

○ Recognizes your talents

○ Embraces your flaws

Oh Dear, I'm Afraid You've Been Duped

Right about now, your Higher Power and expanded POV should be feeling the shock of an awakening—something that feels like the sting of a snapping bra strap, but smacked against your mind rather than your skin. It's true, it's true: Nice Guys deserve a lot more credit than you've given them in the past. In fact, if anyone should steal the "I'm so misunderstood" tagline from Bad Boys, it's the Nice Guy contingent (not that this would ever happen, as few Nice Guys are prone to theft, and Bad Boys will win a whining contest any day). Addickts love challenging Bad Boys with strong backbones and irreverent attitudes—but that doesn't mean a Nice Guy won't reject life's cookie-cutter expectations too.

We wrongly accuse Nice Guys of being better friends than lovers; self-doubting losers who desperately clamor to learn from their smarmy counterparts; and men who are less successful, less ambitious, and have less money than their aggressive peers—among other misconceptions (bookish, weak, insecure . . .). Yet I've met fewer Nice Guys that fit stereotypes than I have Bad Boys who happily copycat theirs. Most Nice Guys I know really like who they are and don't have the time to impress shallow ladies and gents who insist on evaluating them at face or khaki value. And while they're also reputably patient and altruistic in the boudoir, they can also be

"I dated a carpenter who asked if he could 'mount my shelves.' It was such a sweet pun that I fell for it—and we had sex on our first date. The relationship lasted about a month, because let's just say he was 'nailing' another woman's. . . . " —Bethany, 22

(continued)

A MEMO TO YOUR FORMER SELF

We've established that you'll need to rely on a Power stronger than wavering self-control to clean up your act for now. So what if that Power's simply your gut instinct? Though you've done a great job suppressing it on rough dates, your gurgling gut's encouraged you to read this far—so it can't be too misguided. Here's how it might compare the pros and cons of a typical night out with both Good and Bad Boys. It's located in your body's core, which basically makes your gut The Boss of You. No wonder it's sending you an official memo . . .

TO: A Not-Yet-Lost Cause
FROM: Your Pushy Gut
RE: Dating Performance Evaluation

Alright, you addickt: I've had enough of your efforts to ignore my wise prodding and drown out my intuition with G&Ts. As your gut, it's my job to mold you into the best person you can be, and that includes weaning you off counterproductive Bad Boys. I'm up to your spleen in disgust.

Here's a quick review of how you act on Bad Boy dates, and what to expect from a future full of Nice Guys. Listen up and you can look forward to a raise—in the standards department, that is.

BAD HABITS TO DITCH	GOOD HABITS TO HITCH
He extends a last-minute dinner invite, and you accept even if you're already midslice.	He calls you by 4 P.M. to confirm a reservation and surprises you with tickets to a show.
You change your jeans three times. You swear he'll recognize them, even if your last date was a month ago.	You pull your skinny jeans from the hamper, and spray them with his favorite perfume.

BAD HABITS TO DITCH	GOOD HABITS TO HITCH
You spend the hour he's late reapplying blush, so you look fresh when he arrives.	You spend the five minutes he's late applying Chapstick. He loves you without makeup.
You agree to extra Parmesan because he loves it. Who cares if you're lactose intolerant?	He orders the salmon to share, because he read that all women need a healthy dose of vitamin E.
You tell yourself the waitress really is just a friend.	You believe the waitress really is just a friend.
You overlook the doorman's knowing glances and his roommate's ambiguous, "Hey . . . you!"	The doorman knows you by name, and your date owns his own apartment.
When he offers a postcoital cig, you'd rather tell him you quit than admit you've never puffed at all.	He lobbies against secondhand smoke in his free time.
You miss a flight to spend one more hour in bed, and pray it's not $200 to change the ticket.	You miss a flight to spend one more hour in bed, because he pays to change your ticket.
You not-so-accidentally leave your thong on his floor to remember you by.	You accidentally leave your thong on his floor, and he returns it washed and ironed.
You call to make sure he's "okay" days later, though you both know he's blowing you off.	He calls you after your date to make sure you know how much fun he had.
You stopped telling friends about him ages ago, because you shouldn't be with him anyway.	You tell one friend about him, because you're angst-free and anything more is superfluous.

surprisingly unabashed and practiced in the sexual technique department. Good or Bad, boys will be boys, after all.

Now I would be lying if I said that there's a secret society of Nice Guys disguised as trendy uber hipsters—but at this point, I hope your dating musts are deeper than a trucker cap. And if you've yet to arrive, then count on this confession: Often-times, a thimble-full of nerd can be a remarkable trait—especially when it puts you in the power seat. No man appreciates a saucy, beautiful, strong, funny, and self-assured woman more than a Nice Guy. Your image bolsters his—and every man likes to know he's trading up. Has a Bad Boy ever made you feel like such a catch with long-term potential? Exactly.

What It Really Means to Settle

Addickts often think that roping a Nice Guy is settling because they associate Nice with cardigan sweaters and 10 P.M. bedtimes. Nice says *walk all over me in your four-inch stilettos*—and not in a hot Asian masseuse fantasy kind of way. Nice is what our mothers married, what tucks in his shirt, what forgives PMS no matter how bitchy we are. Nice says that life doesn't carry the one we want, so we'll take our second choice for half price.

 WARNING: Much like a push-up bra, Bad Boys are a quick fix to an otherwise droopy situation.

Of course, this kind of thinking is why addickts are, well, addickts—because if there's something truly satisfying about dating someone for six months, only to have him introduce you to strangers as his "friend," I'd like to know what it is. To me, settling compels you to ask four coworkers and your dad to send you an e-mail to test if your system's down—because a Bad Boy hasn't reached out. Settling also looks like not remembering your birthday or not picking up the tab for brunch with the family.

Admit it: Every time you date a Bad Boy, you spend 90 percent of the relationship trying to guess his next move or analyze his current one. *Will he ever call me back? What does his slouch mean? How does he know that redhead? Why do his friends leave his life so often? How many women has he been with—and how do I compare?* Unlike a Nice Guy, a Bad Boy can turn a flirty exchange into a full-blown obsession simply by piquing your interest with questions like these that inevitably cause you to question your sanity. And the really elusive ones? They have you at "Hell no." Chances are, you're not even sure when you're genuinely smitten with a Bad Boy because your nerves are on such high alert that you're guaranteed a sigh of relief when he does come around. It's not that Nice Guys don't keep you on your toes, but they seldom do it from a careless or intentional place. In short, Nice Guys are just as selective as you are. And guess what? Their interests are real, with the potential to last longer than it takes to have morning sex but skip the breakfast part. Nice Guys won't settle for less than what they deserve either. So now you have something else in common.

No, You Greedy Twit! You Can't Have It All

Bad Boys and Nice Guys are not mutually exclusive, since one must exist to elevate, trash, or merely reflect off the other. So you might as well end the search for the perfect Bad/Good

"Maybe it's wrong that I hacked my boyfriend's computer. But when I saw that he bookmarked every porn site on the Web, plus kept photos of his busty ex on his desktop, I felt validated." —Arielle, 26

combo, because it's impossible to expect a Bad Boy's desirable qualities to fit into a Nice Guy paradigm. While you will be pleasantly surprised when he challenges you or represents the unknown, for example, a Nice Guy won't do this by remaining deliberately distant or sweeping you into a dangerous world.

So please dismiss the notion of two archetypes squeezed into a single body, because it's hard enough for them to so much as share the same room. I'll never forget the time I went to a seedy ex's apartment to watch the horse races with his friends; naturally, my goal was to positively shine and provoke a little jealousy, if given the chance. So I snagged my good friend Nate, a man who's as smart as he is handsome. His mere presence makes most men puff out their chests in some primal effort I pretend to understand that helps demonstrate a high testosterone level. The best thing about Nate, though, is that he's also a really Nice Guy.

However. Throwing a Nice Guy into a room of Bad Boys was not one of my smartest tactics, basically because Nate was more intimidated than I. He nervously laughed at the wrong times and pretended to know too much about racing. And just when I wanted to hide in the bathtub (curtain pulled), he farted.

How I wish I were kidding.

As you might expect, the Bad Boys began to snicker and taunt my dear friend. Unfortunately, Nate's comebacks were outnumbered by those of his rivals—and any effort we'd collectively made to look cool in the presence of my ex were immediately negated. I was livid. Desperate to make-nice with the guys (and me?), Nate gave his bravado one last try by inviting the mean-spirited men to a strip club and offering to pay for the steaks. Beyond humiliated, I pulled Nate by the arm, said a quick goodbye, and we drove home in silence. The night and my plan mutually stunk.

That's when I learned that Bad Boys and Nice Guys play off each other's foibles and identities, as they strengthen and cower under the influence of one another's traits. Because they're two very different creatures, they actually thrive on their respective differences—though Nate wasn't given much of a chance to prove his merit that night. He was too busy making jokes about his gas leak, and then clamoring to re-establish his rep by inviting everyone out for slabs of meat among half-naked women. Perhaps if the Bad Boys were on Nate's turf, things would have been equally imbalanced—but more partial to my friend's interests.

Which also reminds me: The worst thing an addickt can do is sit in a room with both breeds and inevitably play comparison games. Bad Boys are too practiced in the art of notice-me, and Nice Guys will inevitably look like dopes by comparison. Especially when in other circumstances, they'd shine. Unfortunately, no Higher Power can shield a new BBA from her own image-conscious, judgmental tendencies. If that were an option, you wouldn't be in this mess to begin.

The Tootsie Roll Pop:
A Reformed Bad Boy's Theory

My friend Anthony is a reformed Bad Boy. He's been faithfully engaged, and he's cheated without remorse. He's treated some women like precious gold and tossed others aside as if they were covered in rust. For the two years I've known Anthony, he's been nothing but an absolute doll to me and the women he's dated. Which always made the details of his Bad Boy adventures sound like the stuff of *Rent*-inspired, bohemian fibs—whether he made out with a stranger after a political protest, called his partner to bail him out of DUI jail charges, or had sex with paint-splattered artists on the floor of his studio. It wasn't until I watched Anthony interact with a past fling, which then introduced me to his Nice Guy theory, that I became a believer.

We were walking Anthony's dog when he and I passed a tall, beautiful brunette with two mini schnauzers. "How've you been?" Anthony asked, bending to pet the pooches. The woman stopped. She glared. And then with all the might of her model-thin frame, pulled her pets down the street with a slight sashay. Anthony was quiet.

"What did you do to her?" I asked, a little too anxious to tap his psyche. *I've been that woman,* I thought. *I know her walk too well. . . .*

"I fucked her and didn't call the next day," Anthony said. His eyes were sharp and unfamiliar. "It happened a long time ago, when I wasn't nice to women because I didn't like myself." I wanted to ask a million questions—all of which began with the word "You?" But I let Anthony break the silence, because if you wait long enough, a man usually will.

"I have this theory about Nice Guys," he said. "There's a formula, an equation that women can use to detect whether someone has a good soul. I had to grow into this formula. It didn't used to come naturally."

Tell me more.

"Soft, around hard, around soft," he said, as if it were obvious. "That's the fool-proof formula for finding a Nice Guy." According to Anthony, Nice Guys have a soft exterior that they allow you to penetrate, a façade that makes them accessible. Next, they'll let you reach a more resolute layer that pushes them to achieve and helps them withstand pressure. And finally, a Nice Guy will reveal his soft-natured core. Visually, the formula reminds me of a Tootsie Roll pop with an extra layer of chocolate. "A Bad Boy is the opposite: hard, around soft, around hard," he concluded.

That night, I mentally ran through my past exploits—and you know what? Every Bad Boy I'd ever dated had a hard center, preceded by a soft one, preceded by a hard one. A hard core didn't always make the Bad Boys rude or angry, but it did make them emotionally resistant to softer, kinder gestures like empathy or love. It's a soft core that gives, receives, and understands the warmth upon which caring relationships are built. Which is what Nice Guys are all about.

"So what about you?" I asked Anthony. "Soft, around hard, around soft?" Absolutely, he said. Now, he said. "And if I met that woman for the first time today, and if she knew the equation, we'd be petting her schnauzers right now."

"I worked part-time at a jewelry store during med school. One day, a man came in to look at rings for his fiancée—and asked me out after he found one! To this day, I wonder if they're divorced." —Amanda, 32

Pace Yourself: A Nice Guy's Not Going Anywhere

Hey, I'm the first to admit that a Bad Boy's quick reveal is a damn fine high. There's nothing more satisfying than immediate gratification when it comes to chemical attraction and personal divulging. But the problem with wanting more, more, now, now is that it makes you too available—which can be uninviting to Bad Boys and Nice Guys alike. I don't care if you're 60 and covered in grizzly old wrinkles; you really do have all the time in the world to perfect your shtick. Especially if it leads to a place that's more peaceful than any you've visited at rapid speed. Especially if your future Nice Guy insists on pacing himself.

As I mentioned earlier, a Nice Guy will seem to move more quickly than a Bad Boy—more dates per week, more compliments per hour—but that doesn't mean he's emotionally falling at a desperate or anxious rate. After an exceptionally shmoopy three months of dating my current beau, I turned to him and coyly asked: "Are you falling in love with me?"—a question, mind you, that only an idiot would pose if she weren't certain of the answer. His response: "Um. . . . " Great. Guess who felt like a toad? A month later, however, my boyfriend finally said the three words I'd been waiting to hear—and confirmed my friend's theory about Nice Guys who gather data before declaring their love.

I can't emphasize enough that although you may be tempted to freak out at a Nice Guy's consistent attention and multidate quota, do not assume he's fishing to see whether you'd like to invest in a small island together! He's just showing captive interest. Chances are your future Nice Guy will reveal his values, feelings, and past at a gradual pace—even if he is wooing you a few times a week. If he chooses to slowly connect as my boyfriend did, please don't find it insulting because you're used to Bad Boys who move more quickly in the self-revealing department. Remember: Fast and furious hasn't always been a sign of sincerity in the past. If anything, a Nice Guy's gradual get-to-know you—coupled with carefree dates—will allow you to really learn about his background, personality, and interests at a nonintimidating pace. This will give both of you plenty of time to consider whether you're ultimately compatible.

As a recovering BBA, I also found that a Nice Guy's slow reveal allowed me to push off a serious commitment right away, should I decide that my Nice Guy was the wrong Nice Guy for me. Not that I'd ever condone cheating, but if you do happen to backslide during the fuzzy area of are we/aren't we in the initial stages of dating, you'll shoulder less guilt if your relationship is still undefined. Oh, and before I conclude the whole love's-a-marathon-and-not-a-sprint lesson: A Nice Guy's well-intentioned detachment also builds curiosity with each satiating date and makes you hungry for more of his time. Believe it or not, your appetite actually doubles when you know more than usual about the person you're dying to get to know better.

Chapter 4

Giving It Up

STEP #3: Make a conscious decision to hand your resolve and Friday nights over to the care of positive influences—even if that means spending QT with your little sister.

As you gradually move from Bad to Nice, your BBA baggage may feel a bit too heavy to manage on your own—especially on the rocky road to recovery. Which is why I suggest you bring along a Sherpa, of sorts. She'll help you navigate the recovery process so you can find your way to personal contentment without stopping for a Bad Boy hit en route. Meet: your Sponsor.

It's possible that tweaking addicktive tendencies can make you feel alienated from your old self. After all, the platonic Nice Guys in your world have reintroduced you to zoo visits, Frisbee tournaments, grassy picnics, and even the occasional craft fair (wind chimes, anyone?). In another life, you'd have spent a Saturday afternoon analyzing your Bad Boy date with friends over Bloody Marys, two celery stalks please (*What does he mean by, "Talk to you later"? Is later an hour from now—or three excruciating months?*). But now, you're actually getting to know the joy of swapping bear hugs with new friends you met at a Portland pumpkin patch. The bliss of wearing tweed jackets and Wellies aside, the latter can occasionally feel downright limiting simply because you're not used to it. Squeezing your Nice Guy's hand might help ease the quease when you cross that bridge, but it's not going to save your instincts from revolting against small children at his family reunion—and pretending to like them. Especially when you can't help but fondly recall how The Old You would've taught the tots a few curse words in Pig Latin.

My advice? Don't be so hard on yourself! You've only recently taken the leap into Nice Guy territory and can't be expected to be the only one who cheers on your new love life—even if it turns out to be amazing 99 percent of the time. Because that still leaves 1 percent of your time clock that you can't handle alone. This is exactly why you must find a devoted, reliable Sponsor. Bonus points if she's also great at parties. . . .

 WARNING: When times are tough, a solo decision-making process can be one hell of a hurdle.

Step 3 is about leaning on positive influences for support and guidance. When times are tough, a solo decision-making process can be one hell of a hurdle. Choosing a Sponsor is basically choosing a loyal friend whose self-control outweighs yours—but she must also relate to your specific situation without judgment. Ideally, that also makes her a recovering addickt so you can look to each other for clarity and support. I can't tell you how important it is that your Sponsor's found herself in similar back seats or thrown over comparable kitchen islands with Bad Boys. By helping you move onto smarter emotional decisions, she'll do the same. Relying on a fun but trustworthy friend who knows your weaknesses, respects your strength, and encourages your journey will transform your recovery from drab to done-deal.

You've always looked to friends for morning-after pep talks; but now, you'll need to ring a chum *before* agreeing to rooftop champagne with a smooth talker. Your Sponsor's job is to put your interests before her own and to share your newfound ideals—as well as your long-standing love for midnight cookie dough binges. She must also be accessible at all times: morning, noon . . . and especially after midnight when your hormones really start to rev. Your Sponsor can be your sister, your best friend, a roommate, or even a neighbor (if she still talks to you after sharing a bedroom wall). Just make sure she lacks man-parts. You don't want to risk codependence on a potentially appetizing specimen who might just vibe with your vulnerable spirit and batting eyelashes. Program your female Sponsor's number into your cell, embroider it onto your bra strap, or tattoo it on your wrist. Just make sure her digits are with you at all times.

So Few Bad Boys, So Much Time

You used to devote hour-long IM sessions to analyzing the ellipsis in a cagey ex's e-mail. Ah, the bad old days with the tragically troubled. So what's an addickt to do with her free time now? Well, I'll tell you.

Start by booking your calendar silly with experiences that open you up to the unknown—whether that means becoming a dog walker or throwing lavish weekend brunches. Refurbishing flea market finds, knitting sweaters for Granny, or writing poems for your local press, though swell activities indeed, may be a bit too solitary for your psyche at this point. Now more than ever, you need to be around animated personalities and moving objects—just to remind yourself that your mind and spirit are in constant motion and that you'll never be stuck in a going-nowhere lifestyle again. Though you've welcomed Nice Guys into your life, yet are still acclimating to what that really means, it's also imperative to keep your most eccentric, audacious, and sharp-tongued friends close to your side. Hopefully your Sponsor possesses a lot of these qualities, so you don't feel too alienated from your comfort zone.

As a recovering addickt, you know how easy it is to get swept into a man's world. But when you become swept into that of a Nice Guy, his universe may seem so foreign—no matter how much you enjoy it—that you risk losing touch with your old interests and personalities, which will only cause you to freak out. Whether we're talking about your present (a Nice Guy friend) or future (a Nice Guy boyfriend), a Nice Guy's idea of a good time will expectedly diverge from yours. The zoo trips and pumpkin patch visits I talked about earlier are fantastic experiences, but when they're your *only* exposure to what defines a "social life," you may risk disconnecting from and floating above your real self—rather than remaining grounded and in touch with your evolving persona, thanks to the support of positive influences.

(continued)

"I dated a man who hurled everywhere but the toilet when he got drunk. My laundry basket full of clean clothes, my closet, the hamper, my nightstand. . . ."
—Elizabeth, 27

THINGS TO DO (INSTEAD OF MEN)

Just as ex-smokers like to munch celery or chew gum, recovering addickts need activities that help fill restless hours otherwise spent fighting withdrawal symptoms. Tempted to dial an old flame? Type an old-fashioned letter during work hours instead! Dying to feel stubble scratch your cheek? Invite friends over to exfoliate with a honey almond scrub! Your goal is to stay busy, so you don't get busy. Now stop whining, and start moving.

IF YOU'RE DYING TO:	DON'T DO IT! TRY:
Reread flirty IMs to remind yourself you've still got it	Joining a book club of women less attractive than you
Cradle a stranger's face in your bosom	Candy striping in the maternity ward of a local hospital
Smell tobacco on a man's fingertips	Finding a hairstylist who's meticulous when cutting asymmetrical bangs
Show-off your new silk teddy to a captive audience	Wearing it with jeans to a party
Accidentally bump into easy targets at regular hang-outs	Training for a triathlon with a gang of fitness mavens

IF YOU'RE DYING TO:	DON'T DO IT! TRY:
Solicit a stranger's hot breath on your neck	Riding public transportation for a week
Stare down a naked man with a lax attitude	Taking a life-drawing class
Run your tongue over a strategically placed tattoo	Volunteering to lick stamps for a nonprofit organization
Clean out the dark corners of a Bad Boy's psyche	Helping clean out the dark corners of your roommate's closet
Feel entirely unappreciated by those who profess to care	Inviting your family to your apartment for the weekend

Although you need to shed your addicktive skin, you don't want to neglect who you were as a person before you began this self-improvement project. When I first began spending time with Nice Guys—and only Nice Guys—during the initial stages of recovery, I was proud to say I could actually become amused by a cage full of monkeys or a *Three's Company* marathon party. But after a few weeks, I felt like I'd completely suppressed elements of myself that helped define me as, well, me: A love for experimental art, the chutzpah to crash a fancy fete in old sneakers, the careless attitude that made me undress in front of open windows. While some of these scenarios invited Bad Boy encounters at one time, a lot of them did not—but I refused to engage entirely for fear that any reference to my past would push me toward a bender. Because tattered Adidas and renegade creatives reminded me of my addickted lifestyle, I avoided them altogether—which, unfortunately, included alienating all Bad Boy friends from my life, who were perfectly capable of playing the role of a platonic plus-one. This was a hasty decision.

 WARNING: Your Sponsor must lack man-parts. You don't want to risk codependence on an appetizing specimen who might just vibe with your vulnerable spirit and batting eyelashes.

What I soon realized was that just because an addickt is working her brassy little tail off to eliminate Bad Boy bologna from her intimate life, I wouldn't recommend that she extricate herself from every one of their outer circles. This doesn't mean contacting a Bad Boy ex and suggesting a friendship reunion, just in time for a George Grosz retrospective. Instead: Remember the guy you never wanted to date but who invited you to rollerblade through his friend's giant loft when he was house-sitting? Or the one who took you on a historic graveyard tour for Halloween? Or the sweet pea who shared his insider knowledge on outsider art? Incorporate them into your social agenda. Because if you're only spending time with Nice Guys, you're probably not getting that stranger-than-fiction fix that Bad Boys satiate. And by diversifying your clique, you'll stimulate your mental, creative, spiritual, and emotional sensibilities—and remind yourself of the good parts of your nutty past that you'd never want to abandon because they helped define a lot of the good things about who you are. Part of the problem with an addicktive lifestyle is that it's so incredibly myopic. Don't fall into a single-minded trap again—but this time, in reverse. Do, however, invite your Sponsor along for the ride to play it safe as often as possible.

One last word of advice: Try not to let the pendulum swing too drastically in one direction or the other. Balance the time you spend with Nice Guy and Bad Boy friends to inevitably feel the most complete. No matter what you choose to do and with whom, I'd avoid mixing extreme Nice Guys with Bad Boy pals until you reach Step 5 and have a more secure handle on your ID. Remember the awkward moment with Nate's bloated intestine? I wouldn't wish that experience on anyone.

Chapter 5

I'm Good Enough, I'm Hot Enough …

STEP #4: Take a brave, probing look at your innermost smut—and admit to yourself, a Higher Power, and another person the juicy details of your honest mistakes.

In most 12-step programs, the process of examining your angst and then confessing your snafus to a party of three are separate, consecutive steps. But for our purposes, I've combined them because I really do think they're as intertwined as two dogs in heat. Plus, so much brain-busting, gut-wrenching self-reflection can be a real buzzkill if we linger on the topic too long—and I prefer to look forward, as much as we look back.

So far, the process of slowly integrating Nice Guys into your world, as you usher out their deceptive foils, has likely had its ups and downs. You've pulled close at one moment, and then pulled away at others. To a Nice Guy who's more stable than a four-post bed, you may look like a sexy schizophrenic with a few identity issues . . . but no matter. Nice Guys will always stick around to eke out the real you, and novelty is always a plus in relationships with good cores—romantic or otherwise.

Most imperative is that you fully exorcise your Bad Boy demons so you can clearly define the life you want to lead before you want to run away from yourself. Unfortunately you can't really move ahead without digging through your past.

Layers upon gooey layers of residual yuck from years as a BBA have found temporary lodging in your pretty little head, heart, and soul. It's time to roll up your sleeves and clean house.

Kiss Your Past Goodbye*

To really dissect your innermost thoughts, feelings, and recreational trappings is to confront a side of yourself that you'd otherwise hide beneath a plunging neckline and waterproof mascara. But why make emotional excavation a tear-jerking experience if we can help it? It's quiz time again, but on this go-round, I need you to apply your most obnoxious red lipstick as heavily as you did as a 10-year-old playing dress-up. You were a minx-in-training then, and you're an addickt in recovery now. Funny how life (or at least lipstick) comes full circle.

In any event, on the following pages are a list of phrases that have crossed your mind or spilled from your alluring mouth as a BBA—and don't you deny it. Instead, rate each quote on a scale of one to five, based on how often you've said or thought the below—and mark your rating with a big kiss mark. That's right, lip smack the paper like it's Tommy Lee's right nipple. Under each familiar quote is space for personal rants that the exercise might solicit. By the time you've finished the exercise, you'll have 1) worn off your smut-stick; 2) purged your past; 3) covered this page with enough confusing memories to warrant tearing it into shreds—and never looking back.

*If the spirit moves you, feel free to go deeper on your own. This list might just be the starting point you need for weekly self-evaluations or Dear Diary entries. Don't forget to hide the key. . . .

"What do you mean, 'There are no new messages in my mailbox?!'"

....

....

....

....

"If I talk dirty, will he hurry up and finish?"

....

....

....

....

"I'm a strong and independent woman!"

....

....

....

....

"If I buy bagels before he wakes up, he'll hopefully stay for breakfast. ... "

....

....

....

....

"Oh no, Mr. Room Service Waiter. I'm not his Mrs. . . . "

....

....

....

....

"It's too soon to use his toothbrush and I can't find my gum. . . . "

....

....

....

....

"Who buys condoms in bulk? And stores them in his kitchen cabinet?"

....

....

....

....

"*Cosmo* says vanilla-scented candles rev hormones. . . . I'll take four."

....

....

....

....

"But he signed his e-mail *xox!*"

....

....

....

....

"Well, you're here and we are drunk...."

....

....

....

....

"When was the last time you changed these sheets?"

....

....

....

....

"Are you my boyfriend?"

....

....

....

....

"Should I say I'm having fun—or does that seem like I'm having too much fun?"

....

....

....

....

"Did he mean to put his finger there?"

....

....

....

....

"Dammit. I hope he didn't see *The Power of Now* on my nightstand."

....

....

....

....

"Is it a bad sign that he smells like single malt when he picks me up?"

....

....

....

....

"How much pubic hair is too much?"

....

....

....

....

....

....

....

"No Mom, I can't ask him to be my wedding date."

....

....

....

....

....

....

....

"If I buy him a Paul Smith wallet, he'll think I want to have his children."

....

....

....

....

....

....

....

"You're perfect. Isn't it funny how life works out?"

....

....

....

....

....

....

"Do you love me?"

....

....

....

....

....

....

Share, and Share Alike

What was once your best party line is about to become an emotionally cleansing activity. Since you've made peace with your addicktive exploits, it's now time to share them with that Higher Power we talked about earlier—and a trusted someone else (preferably your Sponsor). Admitting how you once sucked a Bad Boy's toes to prove how much you liked his Converse or cooked an ex dinner after slicing his old leather jacket into a revealing apron have coined you A Good Time in more than a few circles. Past experiences have helped define your character, sense of humor, and future priorities. Even if they've chipped away at your heart, you're on the road to a more complete you—and completely wiping your past from your memory isn't only impossible, it's undesirable. If you rebuke your previous self so adamantly, you are essentially chiding your spirit for who you once were. And darling, you weren't a bad person by any stretch. Kicking your addickt tendencies simply means you're growing up and ready to move on to a new life phase.

 WARNING: Addickts go through withdrawal symptoms just like any other compulsive eater, gambler, smoker, or drinker. As this affects you, let's just say it won't be a Cover Girl moment.

Healthy self-preservation is a good thing, but why hoard all gatekeeper responsibilities yourself? Sharing your adventures with two other beings—one spiritual, one tangible—will help hold you accountable on various levels. Upon hearing your tawdry tales, these influences will become intimately familiar with each experience so they can look for rebound warning signs and intervene, if necessary. They'll also have a greater sympathy for your journey from Bad Boys to Nice Guys, because you'll have already worked through a lot on your own and can help fill in blanks that might not have been as obvious to you before.

And just like that, your support system has become a zillion times stronger. Yes, a zillion.

 WARNING: Layers upon gooey layers of residual yuck from years as a BBA have found temporary lodging in your pretty little head, heart, and soul.

Because you don't want loved ones to mistake heartfelt confessions for boastful diatribes, keep your bawdy tales brief but detailed—and emotionally informative. Take a hint from talk show therapy by starting potentially shocking stories with "I feel . . . " to lower the weirdness factor to your audience. By saying how you feel, you'll reinforce that you own your opinions, memories, and emotions and aren't afraid of vulnerability. Be sure to intersperse apologies where necessary, but keep the sap factor under control. "Sponsor, I'm sorry I repeatedly abandoned you at seedy bars in the name of meeting Bad Boys elsewhere" is much more appropriate than, "Hey Sponsor! Remember the time we got trashed at that dive and you could hardly stand, but I totally left you alone just so I could make out with that bearded freak in his Mom's basement? Sucked to be you! Sorry, babe." Use sympathetic cue cards to help with talking points, if need be. I suggest striped index cards—the pink kind, just because.

"After a first date, I took this guy back to my apartment to make out. I'm a natural C-cup, and when he lifted my shirt, he said, 'Suh-weet!' What an awful frat boy response—especially from a thirty-two-year-old." —Rachel, 28

Since your entire repertoire of Bad Boy stories won't flood your brain in one sitting, you may have to repeat Step 4 at various intervals. As you experience a heavy verbal flow, you'll enter a state of detox—which is intended to clean your entire being from germy guys. It won't be pretty, but once it's over, you'll have never felt better.

Derelict Detox: Stressing! Puking! Dancing!

If your Sponsor's good at her job, she won't be afraid to grab a Bad Boy's wrist from your grip—and replace it with a Nice Guy's palm, if not her own. But that's not where her responsibilities end. Whether they're binge daters or have established long-term Bad Boy patterns, addickts go through withdrawal symptoms just like any other compulsive eater, gambler, smoker, or drinker. And as this affects you, let's just say it won't be a Cover Girl moment.

The disconcerting news is that as you flush your fondness for Bad Boys from your body, withdrawal symptoms surface in relation to decreasing amounts of attraction and even saliva. (This is why so many addickts insist on having a morning romp to steady their nerves or calm anxiety.) To properly detox, lock yourself in a room with your Sponsor and spew every last secret, desire, and anecdote remotely related to living as a BBA. Come clean about the time you spent the night with a Park Avenue stranger, just so you could wake to a great view of the Metropolitan Museum of Art! Confess that you took mom's Saturday morning call while stroking the lightning bolt tattoo on a man's inner thigh! When pushing Bad Boy blech out of your system, it's important to stay well-hydrated and rest in a dark, quiet room. This last part goes for your Sponsor, too, since she'll be the one listening to your stories for the 928th time and dabbing your face with a damp cloth.

The detox period is mildly uncomfortable but will disappear after a short period of tension, restlessness, headaches, distress, and insomnia. Sweaty palms, nausea, and increased heart rates are extreme symptoms, though not unheard of. Given that addickts spend so much time in dark, smoky bars, they might flinch at light that looks shockingly bright or smells that are especially pungent.

Once you've exhausted both your and your Sponsor's nerves, it's extremely important to end with a smile. After sweating and vomiting away Bad Boy detritus, I can't think of anything more satisfying than doing a little dance . . . with props! All you need is Bad Boy memorabilia (hats, photos, toothbrushes, Play Stations), a flaming trash can, and a good amount of rhythm. Sing with me, now—to the tune of "The Hokey Pokey":

> *You put his CD case in*
> *But take the CDs out*
> *You add his favorite boxers*
> *And resist the urge to pout*
> *You do the Derelict Detox*
> *And you turn your life around*
> *That's what it's all about!*

Chapter 6

Playing Nice

STEP #5: You're absolutely, positively, bet-your-Louboutins-on-it convinced that you're ready to move past Addickt character flaws . . . and on to Nice Guy investments.

So far, you've opened yourself up to Nice Guys—though the extent to which you've allowed them to penetrate your day-to-day will vary from one BBA to another. It's important that you also begin to take responsibility for your actions, if just in baby steps, because you can hold a Higher Power and Sponsor responsible for your well-being for only so long. It's officially your job to move past BBA mannerisms once and for all.

Like seltzer in your cranberry juice, it's refreshing to know that a Nice Guy will make this process easy on you—whether he turns out to be a friend, flirt, fling, or true love in the long run. I never recommended hopping from the back of a Bad Boy's bike and onto the pillowed daybed of a Nice Guy—playful and ready for all things saucy. You can't expect a man to rescue you, if you haven't rescued yourself. But if I've said it once: Having Nice Guys as boy friends (Two words, sugar! Two words.) does cushion the transition—a transition you're now ready to make. At this point in the program, it's time to take your biggest step yet. . . .

Dust off that diaphragm and get ready to date again!

If you're a teensy bit leery about allowing Nice Guys to play the romantic lead in your life, don't get frustrated on me now. When you were a child and learned to read, your first grade teacher convinced you that everyone moves at her own pace. She suggested you sound out words, and that you understand the pronunciation of every letter, contraction, and consonant blend before allowing them to roll off your tongue. Ditto for dating. By now, you know the Nice Guy basics and what to expect from each—both because of this primer and your real life encounters with Nice Guys. It's okay to take your time with each new dating prospect, and incorporate the introspection and real-life savvy you've gathered thus far into your routine.

 WARNING: Nice Guys are just as capable of pulling away, redefining boundaries, and feeling cornered as Bad Boys.

When my Nice Guy boyfriend and I started seeing each other, I wasn't convinced that he was the right guy for me. He told too many jokes, wore mauve woolly sweaters, and only ate at restaurants within a five-block vicinity of his apartment. This was a triple-yuck factor, in my book. But Nice Guy friends and my Sponsor offered encouragement ("Take him to Barneys!" "Introduce him to Nobu!"), and on our fifth date, all I noticed was how much this Nice Guy sparkled from the inside-out. And as each year passes, he continues to impress me: with how much he sacrifices for his family, how humble he is about his talents, how he dispenses advice to friends—and most importantly,

"When my husband goes on a business trip, he sends me exotic flowers every day— and he often has them waiting in hotels when I'm away too." —Karen, 30

never pressures me to move faster than I'm ready. Believe me: Everyone who meets us immediately comments on how incredibly different we are, with contrasting interests and opposite opinions. Yet the values that keep us together are those that a Nice Guy upholds—and that as a recovering BBA, I've learned to really appreciate. Learned, my friends, is the key word here. And just like learning to read: Patience is fundamental.

Once your Nice Guy love life is off and running, dateworthy men will feel like redemption personified; just being around them makes you feel cherished, acknowledged, and absolved of Bad Boy sins. They have a knack for swooping in at just the right moment to cook you dinner, wipe your tears, walk your dog, sing you songs, buy you presents . . . and the list goes on. Sometimes the treat's a surprise, and sometimes you have to ask for it—but regardless, I've found that BBAs are 1) seldom afraid to make the request; and 2) seldom disappointed when a Nice Guy delivers. The best part about this is not the delicious outcome: Roasted chicken and diamond solitaires are only so rewarding. It's the fact that you feel safe enough to ask for what you want, have faith that your need will be met—and then bubble over with pleasure when it's met exceptionally well. Your Nice Guy feels like a Knight in Well-Pressed Denim—and granted, a lot of this is relative. Bad Boys either never bothered to go the extra mile or simply weren't hardwired to put others first. Sure, they'd occasionally tie on a cape and call themselves a hero—but not long after you took flight, you crashed into a pile of shit. Don't count on that now.

Of Course, Nice Guys Are Not Fault-Free

Remember when fat-free cookies hit the market, and you couldn't help but stuff yourself with six at once instead of the serving size of two? After all, they didn't contain fat—and fat is no friend of a woman's hips. It didn't take long, however, to learn that eating too many fat-free items could still add pudge because fat-free works only in moderation. Similarly, Nice Guys are not fault-free. No matter how many redeeming qualities they have, we can't expect Nice Guys to provide an easy answer to our woes—and overindulgence (time spent, calls made, cheeks kissed) has the potential to disappoint and burst our expectation bubble.

If you were an innate pro at managing expectations, you wouldn't be a recovering BBA. When you dated Bad Boys, you threw expectations out with last year's Uggs. The only things you could rely on with these guys were that 1) their attentive high would feel amazing while it lasted; and 2) they would consistently disappoint you. But now that you're mingling with Nice Guys, feel free to articulate your needs—and try not to act too surprised when they're consistently met. Every once in a while, though, Nice Guys are just as capable of pulling away, redefining boundaries, and feeling cornered as Bad Boys. The difference is that their conscience has a much shorter turn-around time. Nice Guys will spaz without warning because they're only human, and it's unrealistic to expect them to be perfect all the bloody time. But that's okay, because their "Count on me . . . but not too much" attitude reinforces that they're not your spineless bitch—which is a notoriously attractive quality in any person, Good or Bad. They don't want to be set up to deliver unrealistic precision, because that leaves a window for you to overreact to their flaws. And Nice Guys really do hate to disappoint.

 WARNING: Truly revealing yourself to a Nice Guy is somehow less daunting than stripping down to your skivvies.

You already know how the story ends, but when I first allowed my Nice Guy to skinny dip in my dating pool, I couldn't get over how well he understood my eccentric family, health concerns, bizarre friends, and shoe obsession—with true blue empathy and interest. Compared to the Bad Boys I'd met who peed in my sink when they were drunk or laughed at my mother's quirks rather than tried to understand them, this guy seemed heaven-sent once we hit the three-month mark. Six months into the relationship, my expectations were through the roof—and though I never told my Nice Guy that I'd already named our children and mentally decorated our renovated loft, he saw it in my big brown eyes. One night after we perfected a few moves from his *Kama Sutra* book, my Nice Guy sang me a song he'd written—and we played the "I love you!"/"I love you more!" game until we nearly made ourselves puke.

"You're perfect," I said, with a sigh of bewilderment and appreciation.

And that's when the moment died.

Several silent minutes later, my Nice Guy explained that he *never* wanted to hear me call him that again. Perfect is an idealization, he reasoned. Perfect creates expectations. We don't say perfect, or else we risk disappointment.

At first, I was confused. How could imperfections be sexy in Bad Boys, but annoying in Nice Guys? Yet my boyfriend knew enough about my psyche to realize what I didn't: that Nice Guy flaws would seem twice as upsetting to me because I wouldn't expect to see them coming.

That said, continue to trust your man but realize that the Nice Guy is bound to eventually trouble you with inconsistencies and frustrations of his own. This is yet another reason why you're responsible for building your self-image and locating your center, first and foremost. Higher Powers, Sponsors, and patient roommates should become support systems, not lifelines.

Nice Guy Perk-You-Ups

The last thing you need to do is dwell on Nice Guy disappointments. Letdowns were the reason you ditched Bad Boys in the first place. Though all Nice Guys weren't created equal, they do share the following archetypal perks that promise a hot and bothered partnership. Are you ready to replace your drippy doubts with saucy shockers? As a BBA, I know there's very little you like more than recognizing personality traits that defy preconceptions. . . . Let the swooning begin.

DRIPPY DOUBT:	If you suggest a hot club, he'll think you mean a Dungeons & Dragons convention in New Mexico.
SAUCY SHOCKER:	He was a DJ during college and can dirty dance like it's 1987. "I carried a watermelon" will become your favorite cheeky euphemism in no time.

DRIPPY DOUBT:	He'll wear tight white underwear or boxers that feature mice chasing cheese.
SAUCY SHOCKER:	He's been free-balling since he was thirteen years old.

DRIPPY DOUBT:	His perfect posture from military school foreshadows rigid skills as a lover.
SAUCY SHOCKER:	His West Point education promises he'll know how to take direction, salute your body, and find your G-spot as if it were a covert operation.

DRIPPY DOUBT:	He'll have the same friends since high school, which screams "anti-social."
SAUCY SHOCKER:	He has the same friends since high school, which screams "fiercely loyal."

DRIPPY DOUBT:	His PDA will be turned on at all times, ready to beam info to his nerdy techno-buddies.
SAUCY SHOCKER:	You'll turn him on at all times, and he'd kill to beam you after a little PDA. . . .

DRIPPY DOUBT:	He drives a hybrid car, which means he'll probably decorate his walls in Greenpeace posters, too.
SAUCY SHOCKER:	Environmentalism can be a sexy thang. At least Pierce Brosnan and Leonardo DiCaprio think so. . . .

DRIPPY DOUBT:	He'll be bookish and bright, but not exactly a boardroom tiger.
SAUCY SHOCKER:	Who cares? You've never picked up a check.

DRIPPY DOUBT:	His blackheads will be worse than yours.
SAUCY SHOCKER:	There's lots of fun to be had in bed with Bioré strips and a damp cloth. Oh, admit it. You know you're a squeezer too.

DRIPPY DOUBT:	He'll collect *Star Wars* action figures, though puberty is a distant memory.
SAUCY SHOCKER:	If you do the math, it only takes three vintage Luke Skywalkers, two boxed Han Solos, and one Peter Mayhew autographed Chewbacca to fund airfare costs for a topless vacation in Nice—thanks to the kids at eBay.

DRIPPY DOUBT:	He'll let peers and family walk all over him.
SAUCY SHOCKER:	He supports peers and family, no matter what their shoe size.

| DRIPPY DOUBT: | He could never whip up a meal that didn't involve spaghetti in a can. |
| SAUCY SHOCKER: | "Naked Chef," anyone? |

| DRIPPY DOUBT: | His Ph.D. in robotics means he'll spend nights in the lab. |
| SAUCY SHOCKER: | His Ph.D. in robotics means he spends nights in the lab programming your vibrator to bring you hot coffee in the morning. |

Hey Missy, You Have Some Explaining to Do

To fully transition from naughty to nice, you not only have to be honest with yourself about your intentions—but you need to be real with any Nice Guy you meet. As a BBA, you could get away with revealing only a smidge of your friendship circle, funny bone, or family life . . . and tweak the rest to a Bad Boy's liking or carve out a new identity for yourself without him calling your bluff. Too bad Nice Guys have higher expectations for you and your relationship than their careless counterparts. I'm not saying Nice Guys are apt to race down the aisle, but they will want to cut right to the heart of who you are simply because they're invested. Believe it or not, they're much more selective than Bad Boys about the women with whom they share their time. Nice Guys aren't out for a disingenuous connection when they can have the real thing; in fact, anything less will likely throw them off course since they don't often take risks on women who aren't sincere.

If you let Nice Guys peek into your true soul, they'll be hooked at "My name is. . . . " Whether their reveal is slow or fast, it's the most pure version of an "I'll show you mine, if you show me yours" exchange.

The truth is, truly revealing yourself to a Nice Guy at any pace is somehow a less daunting task than stripping down to your skivvies. But this should feel less scary when you remind yourself that a Nice Guy's intentions are about acing You 101 before he graduates to the next level of togetherness. (For example, I've known Nice Guys to wait up to three months to have sex for the first time. Wow, I know!) In any case, you'll eventually need to tell him about your BBA tendencies because they're such a part of your dating past and current personality—and God forbid he find out from your snickering friends or via an accidental run-in with an intimidating ex. Both of which could end very, very badly.

A quick tip: Only divulge snippets once you've established weeks of trust together—and in an organic fashion. Blurting out, "A man once drank Veuve Clicquot from my belly button!" after having tipsy sex with your Nice Guy is not a swift move. Start with general revelations and gradually move to specific anecdotes, as you gauge his response to each story. If you notice that he bristles, do not become defensive;

"Without saying a word about being cold, my live-in boyfriend often brings me a blanket when we're watching TV at night. We live in the mountains, so he does this a lot." —Jenny, 29

understandably, it may take your Nice Guy a minute to be okay with the fact that the wonderful woman he adores is the same one who spent Naked Sundays with a man whose last name she never knew. But don't worry, he'll come around.

The flip side is that because of your BBA status, a Nice Guy may always wonder if you'll backslide into the past—or worse yet, that he'll never measure up himself. This could be an emotional, sexual, or physical precaution. Don't become impatient with his timeline and potentially incessant questioning; for the most part, you're both in uncharted territory. In all cases, it's your job to reassure your Nice Guy that you like where and who you're becoming—which includes spending time with him.

To quiet both your fear of judgment and his fear of abandonment, I suggest meeting for coffee to discuss deal-breaking issues that might arise in your future—within the first few weeks of realizing that he's long-term potential. Adopt a gentle tone, then fire away: How often does he expect to see you? How does he feel about the other men in your life? Does your past make him uncomfortable? By meeting at a coffee shop, you're not in a physically compromising position (in bed) or emotionally tenuous situation (feeling angry or confused). Starbucks is neutral territory with mass-produced blueberry loaf; there's nothing threatening about this joint.

Listen for subtexts in each other's deal-breaking index, and ask questions that branch out from these. If he expects you to spend time with his family three times a month, and you don't even visit yours three times a year, lay these cards on the table from the start—and explain why building a strong foundation, without too much parental influence, is important to you. Your conversation will successfully unravel relationship mysteries because it's guided by open, honest communication. Step 6 specifically deals with interpreting speech, so I won't waste my breath here on reading tone or interpreting language.

What I will say is that before your lattes are cold, I guarantee you'll have reached an initial comfort zone with each other's boundaries, priorities, and histories. Just please resist the urge to lick the frothy head off your coffee as your Nice Guy's spilling his heart out. It will only reinforce predatory preconceptions.

Chapter 7

What Did You Just Call Me?

STEP #6: Humbly ask your Nice Guy to be patient with your limitations. This includes developing a relationship vernacular in which you won't confuse "I love you" with "Add me to your 401(k)."

You, your Sponsor, and your Higher Power have joined forces like an Unholy Trinity to remove shortcomings from your conscience and psyche. Though your BBA recovery requires regular check-ins and upkeep, you should be proud of yourself for developing a solid bond with a Nice Guy! After you've connected about your past, ask him to be patient with your limits and deal breakers. The key to any healthy relationship is to be specific when expressing your needs and understanding his. And because communication is everything, Step 6 explores adoring expressions—and how to throw them around like a well-adjusted pro (without feeling stifled, insecure, or uncomfortable).

Attaching monikers to one's identity like "commitment" or "girlfriend" may be a breeze for your sweetheart, but for a seasoned Bad Boy dater with potential tryst issues? Not always. Bad Boys taught you that open and vulnerable meant easy access to the fetal position blues, which is why you may have trouble letting down your guard with a Nice Guy. Take heart! Your cagey nature is only temporary—and your Nice Guy will honestly get it, even if you only give him a top-line explanation. He's good like that.

On the other hand, your Nice Guy may have no problem putting *his* thoughts and feelings on the table. He won't mush before he's ready, but there's a 97 percent likelihood that he'll be authentic every step of the way (stats vary according to age, hairline, and penis size). Against your usual instincts, please try to take a Nice Guy's words at face value, because I promise that this one has no reason to cloak his intentions. Don't let his candidness intimidate you.

Of course, don't take a Nice Guy's playful jabs or comments made without a filter cap too lightly either—especially when your quips and his responses act as crib notes to recognizing each other's secret hang-ups. Thankfully, touchy scenarios initiate dialogue—which only brings you closer. Compared to your exes, Nice Guys have an extraordinary threshold for complex and murky discussions. But Nice Guys are also not saints, and at some point, they do have the potential to snap like dead ends after too many hours between a straightening iron.

Suspect a disagreement's mounting? Confront the situation and your needs head on, and at an ASAP rate—but don't beat a dead horse. Even Nice Guys have their limits for Relationship OCD. For example, if you need emotional reinforcement about whether your Nice Guy really meant it when he joked about sleeping his way to the top of his female-run company, limit your inquisitions to two rounds of Q&A. Make sure you go deeper the second time, so you're expanding upon ideas and not repeating them. The last thing you want to hear a Nice Guy say is, "I thought I already explained. . . . " Tell him exactly what you need him to say to calm your nerves—whether it's "I love you" four times a day or "My boss smells like dead flowers" after a company retreat. Give your Nice Guy a formula that makes it easy to make you cheerful, and there's a good chance he'll follow it to ease everyone's mind. Extraordinarily so, your goals are his.

AN ADDICKTIONARY OF TERMS

Back when Bat Girl Underoos were the closest thing you owned to a matching bra and panty set, you probably spent Monday through Thursday studying for a big vocabulary quiz on Friday. Not only did you have to know how to spell each word, but you had to understand its meaning within the context of a sentence. Whether you scored a gold star or a frown face, these words helped you collectively define your world.

Now imagine what would happen if at the peak of your development, you were told by coercive and trustworthy peers that every word's meaning had a second meaning. Or that its meaning could change, depending on who used it. Or that some words, in fact, had no meaning at all.

If this were the case, I personally would have spent more hours scaling imaginary walls in my Underoos than cramming for those quizzes. Why bother to learn the rules if they would always change? Similarly, BBAs have been deprogrammed by Bad Boys to misunderstand relationship semantics—and in many cases, not use them at all. The whole process kind of made you commitment challenged. And you thought the only special bus you deserved to ride was the one you slept in as a Ryan Adams groupie. . . .

Because there's no such thing as sign language for the relationship-impaired, you'll need to reintroduce yourself to relationship vernacular to fully engage with a Nice Guy. Expect to be shocked at how many of these words were useless to you as an addickt—but will now play a role in your life as a recovering BBA. The harder you work to memorize these terms, the less you'll stutter or trip over pronunciation. And when put into practice, they won't intimidate, frustrate, confuse, frighten, or escape you any longer.

BED & BREAKFAST: No, not your one-night-stand routine. Someone else's cozy house in which you snooze in another couple's bed, eat their home-made muffins, and compliment their family photos. It's like staying at your grandparents' home—if they were complete strangers.

BOYFRIEND: You will call your Nice Guy this to friends and family, mostly when he's not around, to remind yourself that you're no longer an unattached floozy.

BUDWEISER GIRLS: He won't own the collector's edition of their hot tub promotional ad, but you may catch him bidding online just for fun. Take it as a sign that he'll look, but never touch.

CANOODLE: Forget Grope Fest 2006. This kinder, gentler PDA is your nuzzle of choice.

COMMITMENT: An agreement between two lovebirds not to date other hotties, no matter how much red wine and steak frites are involved. No really, people do this.

COMMUNICATION: This keeps him coming back for more. He wants to understand you.

FLANNEL: A cuddly alternative to exposing skin, especially during PMS. And he won't think you're any less sexy because of it.

GIRLFRIEND: Your Nice Guy will call you this to his friends and family, even when you're not around. He does not use this word because he forgot your name.

HONEY: He'll make you a nervous wreck when he calls you this . . . until you do it back.

LEAF PEEPING: It sounds dirty, but LP is nothing more than voyeurs driving for hours to ooh and aah over foliage. Like apple picking and wine tasting, LP is one of those pastimes you always wished you could do with a patient boyfriend—and now that you have one, it can be a bittersweet yawn. Call it a "special occasion," and limit LP to twice a year.

A LITTLE SOMETHING: Random gifts that prove you're on a Nice Guy's mind. They'll increasingly link to personal experiences—say, a joke about his family or a crass word printed on a T-shirt—as your relationship grows.

PANTY LINES: You'll allow these to occasionally show because Nice Guys are more forgiving of laundry day underwear than thong-loving Bad Boys. Break out the Hanes Her Way. . . .

PASTA: Learn to love it, carbs be damned. Early in your relationship, a Nice Guy will offer to cook—and I'll bet my ever-growing thighs that pasta will be on the menu.

PAYCHECK: A Nice Guy blows his on your birthday gift.

PET: He'll not only offer to feed it when you're away, but he'll teach it new tricks!

POTTERY BARN: Every Nice Guy owns at least one piece of this catalog's furniture. Compliment the generic faux-maple end table and move on.

RESPECT: Experience it, and a Bad Boy's disregard becomes unacceptable.

SINCERITY: A tactic Nice Guys use to reassure you that you do not have cankles.

SNUGGLE: This is a choice, not a post-romp obligation—and may involve twisting yourself into a human pretzel, sometimes in lieu of sex. Clothing optional.

STAY: Because loyalty is paramount, he'll do this whenever you wish.

TOGETHER: You're happiest when you and your Nice Guy are this way.

U-HAUL: Without a complaint, your dear boyfriend will drive this to your parents' home four hours away so you can swap spring clothes for fall. You care about cashmere—and he cares about you, caring about cashmere. Look how well that works out.

After you've committed these words to memory (or at least written them on your hand), give yourself 30 to 60 days to actually believe you deserve for them to become part of your life. Because BBAs are accustomed to relaxed attitudes and limited commitment dialogue ("You're hot!" does not count), your instincts will want to doubt a Nice Guy's vocab. Instead, settle into a headspace without ego, hesitation, or self-punishment—and take a celebratory stroll toward being a better person and partner. Even if it is through a pile of leaves.

WARNING: Couple speak will be part of your new relationship. If you're not a fan, learn to like it.

How to Talk Couple Without Losing Your Cool

Sure, you've talked dirty. But have you ever talked couple? It sounds scarier than it is—and if done correctly, you'll feel that much closer to your Nice Guy. When I first began talking couple, my worst fear was that I'd lose my cool—in both a literal and figurative way. In fact, during the first few months of my Nice Guy partnership, my personal stay-happy trick was for us to act as single as possible (separate friends, separate holidays). I bucked against anything that made me feel stifled, limited, or claustrophobic—and language was on the top of that list. Pet names and speaking in "we" made me want to lose my lunch. The thought of slipping into baby talk set off an instinct to shove a pacifier in my mouth as a preventative measure.

But then I grew up.

For many BBAs, couple talk might as well be a foreign language. Then again, you might be really excited to expand your vocabulary as your Nice Guy attachment matures—and if so, brava. Either way, you must expect that couple speak will be part of your new relationship . . . and if you're not a fan, you'll learn to like it. One of the fun things about dating Bad Boys was that feeling you'd get that you were a special find, chosen among the hotter riff-raff to pose as his one and only. It's almost as if you were on the inside, looking out. Well, translate that feeling to the situation you're in now. Single women are hardly slim pickings, and though we all know you're a prize, don't forget that your Nice Guy has chosen to spend Sunday afternoons with *you* during TBS's romantic comedy lineup. If you can coexist as a unit without losing your identity, then you can talk couple and watch it pull you closer. The trick is in how you define this for yourself.

To avoid spewing insipid drivel, I like to take the inside joke and story route. Talking couple simply means solidifying your relationship with words that help you build a shared language. You don't need to pout as if you were Jessica Rabbit to sex up expressions. Inside stories will unite you because they represent collective memories, humor, and thought processes. Uncover moments that embarrass him, elate you, mock friends—and then exploit each one to color your rapport. Spout generics like "dear" and "sweetheart," and you'll risk sounding like the 1950s suburbanite next door. Why choose gushy pet names like "Pooky" or "Shnookems" when you can call each other by titles that actually mean something? I've nicknamed my Nice Guy "Pigpen" because his apartment could use a good scrub, and my friend Allison has earned the pet name "Bunny" because she's as jumpy as a wild rabbit. It helps to be clever, but it's more important to reference specifics in your connection.

Slipping couple talk into routine moments will also keep things fresh in a familiar way. For

"On our one-year anniversary, my boyfriend took me back to the place we first met. He prepared a candlelit dinner at the very spot where I'd kissed him just 365 days before." —Lisa, 29

example, my Nice Guy very seldom lets me pick up the tab. But one time, we offered to treat my friend Amy to dinner without realizing the restaurant didn't accept credit cards. My Nice Guy was short on cash, so guess who paid? Me—and it wasn't a big deal. But one week later, Amy happened to pass the window of a cheap Chinese restaurant in which we were eating soup . . . just in time to see me throw down my plastic. Now, each time I pay for anything, he and I say in unison, "Hi Amy!" because we expect her to show at a moment's notice. The story's nothing outrageous to an outsider, but to an inside duo, the tale takes on special meaning.

What Happens When *He* Bombs the Vocab Quiz?

Even the nicest of Nice Guys will freeze on cue if you look into his eyes, just three weeks into your relationship, and breathe, "I want to have your babies." I talked earlier about how Nice Guys are not exempt from wanting to move slowly or suppress an instinct to bolt if your relationship becomes exceptionally heavy. The upshot is that they will talk to you about their curiosities because they're seldom erratic souls—and you'll reach a mutual consensus about how you both feel. If your Nice Guy doesn't initiate this chat, you will—because you'll instinctively know that he won't run from the prodding.

Unfortunately, this does not mean that a Nice Guy will never feel cornered. Words can throw him just as easily as they can send you into a mental tizzy. Though I'd never endorse putting your own thoughts on the back burner, it might be easiest on your budding romance if you follow the Nice Guy's lead in tenuous situations. If he speaks in "we," then ditto his tone and context. If he drops the L-bomb, then you know it's safe to do the same when you're ready. This lowers the risk of you 1) watching him startle; 2) questioning his commitment; 3) acting on flight or fight instincts—and calling the relationship off if you don't like his response. BBAs are a sensitive gang thanks to years of push/pull relationships, and the last thing you want to do is doubt yourself because of someone else's timeline differences. If you prefer to be the aggressor, manage expectations. Unlike Bad Boys, who are intense one moment and iffy the next, Nice Guys want to make sure they're not only on the same page before they read from the relationship script—but in the same act, correct scene, and well-fitted costume. Encourage his efforts with touchy feely, positive reinforcement—a kiss on the forehead here, a deep-tissue massage there. Your Nice Guy's working overtime to make you feel secure, so it's only fair that you do the same.

 WARNING: Attaching monikers to your identity like "commitment" or "girlfriend" may be a breeze for your sweetheart, but for a seasoned Bad Boy dater with potential tryst issues? Not always.

Because talking couple can be a challenge, I suggest you practice key phrases when you're in scenarios that lack intensity. The word "love," of course, is the biggest stumper—so I suggest saying it often and with abandon, until both your ears and his are conditioned for the real confession.

I LOVE this tuna melt!

I LOVE imported Persian rugs!

I LOVE talking about how much I LOVE using the word LOVE!

See, just like that.

Chapter 8

Emergency Action

STEP #7: Forgive yourself if you cave. Applaud yourself if you don't. This is a process, girls. A process.

When the Nice Guy rings with his goodnight courtesy call, your heart warms to the familiar sound of his voice. "Don't forget, babycakes! Tomorrow we visit newlywed friends and their two Siamese cats in the gentrified suburbs! There's a Talbots around the corner! We're staying overnight at my parents' house, which will be teeming with extended family anxious to chat about midwives and olive paste recipes!"

Sure thing, you think. *Anything for my Pigpen,* you think. . . .

It's not until you're actually smack in the middle of such a cutesy couple moment that your love life's wake-up call rings loud and clear. Your body and mind alarm, no matter how fast you slam the snooze. Can't breathe? Must be cat dander. Chronic migraine? Probably PMS. When the Nice Guy's nephew yells that the new girl has no boobies, you curse Calvin Klein for not padding his seamless bras. Children. Underwear. Olive paste. Your relationship seemed so peaceful last night. Why is it so overwhelming today?

These are the times that try a BBA's soul.

Right about now, your knee-jerk reaction is to line up a friend with benefits, your best wingman, and a row of Jameson shots at a dingy old haunt—just to remind yourself that you can. You're not wearing a ring. Hell, you're not even wearing underwear. Maybe you need a relationship readjustment, compliments of an unattached someone who won't remember either detail in the morning. Maybe he'll say just the right thing like, "Can I lick your bum later?" which will hurl you back into the open arms of a considerate gent who already knows the answer. Maybe a Bad Boy Rebound will make you cherish your new boyfriend's supreme niceness, simply by not being your supremely nice boyfriend. Maybe. . . .

Not so fast, sister. The way I see it, you have two obvious options here. Consider both before you make a rash and randy decision. That is, assuming you haven't already speed-dialed your cohorts from the bathroom between dinner courses— when you should have been calling your Sponsor.

Option 1: Think with Your Hormones

If your estrogen levels insist on a little hanky panky, I certainly can't stop you—especially if you're experiencing a moment of dire panic or bratty revolt. Just be aware that no matter whom you choose to romp with—whether it's a stranger, ex, or friend—you'll feel a tidal wave of nausea once you notice that you have two missed calls on your cell phone from your Nice Guy and the briefs on your floor belong to someone who uses pomade. My advice? Avoid morning-after weirdness by refusing a sleepover at all costs. Book an hour with your therapist, and stuff your face with a chocolate muffin to muffle really tawdry confessions while enjoying a serotonin rush. For at least the next two weeks, expect to act cagey, needy, and clingy with your Nice Guy; you'll need to feel the validation of his affection to compensate for your guilt. Personally, I've found that watching back-to-back reruns of *Dawson's Creek* is an amazing study tool on how to sleep around and never really face the consequences. Then again, if Jen had a 12-step program like this one, maybe she wouldn't have been so miserable chasing unrequited loves and deadbeat men for six seasons. Joey would have made an excellent Sponsor. . . .

If you're crippled with remorse—and I'd be surprised if you aren't—don't lavish the Nice Guy with gifts or go on a cookie-baking spree. Act the least bit suspicious, and he'll smell a fish before he gets a whiff of your Toll House morsels. Just because your Nice Guy's kind, doesn't mean he's dumb. But since you're dead-set on ruining weeks of work and falling off the wagon, there's no sense in getting caught. Here's how I suggest wiping the guilt and smudged lipstick off your irresistible face, so everyone can move on already:

◆ **Take a hot bath, exfoliate, and whip up a mask.** This will soothe your nerves and remove leftover Bad Boy detritus from your body.

◆ **Trash all condoms.** You don't need your beagle to find one under the bed and mistake it for a rubber chew toy. Who's up for a game of fetch? Definitely not your Nice Guy.

◆ **Put a two-person maximum on post-romp analysis.** One of these people should be your Sponsor. Last night's snafu should not become cocktail banter. No matter how good he was.

◆ **Meditate on why you flung in the first place.** How do you plan to avoid future encounters? Fool a Nice Guy once, shame on you. Fool him twice . . . it's over. If anyone has integrity, it's a Nice Guy.

◆ **Buy new sheets.** Otherwise, you'll mentally revisit the affair every time you climb into the striped bedding that swallowed you whole. Worst-case scenario, you'll grow to hate pinstripes altogether. And there's no reason Wamsutta should suffer too.

◆ **Initiate a quiet night with the Nice Guy.** This will serve as a reminder of what real intimacy looks, feels, smells, and sounds like. Memorize this experience. You'll be straddling each other in no time.

I do want to be clear about one thing: I am not encouraging you to show off a fresh Brazilian wax to a Bad Boy lover. I'm simply saying that if you need to dip your toe back into the murky man pool to either satisfy a craving, prove you've still got it, or confirm that you're on the right Nice Guy track—one (albeit fabulous) program can't compete with your will.

 WARNING: Your knee-jerk reaction might be to line up a friend with benefits, your best wingman, and a row of Jameson shots at a dingy old haunt—just to remind yourself that you can.

You've also spent years juggling men who've been anything but devoted to one woman, which is why I also encourage you to wait longer than usual to commit to a Nice Guy. His behavior can be so foreign to a BBA that it's not unusual for you to flirt with your past while tweaking your dating future. What really matters is whether you've resolved whatever question you needed to answer by fooling around. If so, your fling wasn't a complete waste of saliva.

READY TO BLOW?

Mixing edgy moments with bad men can be a toxic combo. You know your defenses are weak when . . .

◆ The Nice Guy rings his landlord about a broken toilet, and you find it curiously hot that the old man never calls back.

◆ The Nice Guy invites you to a family picnic, and you become fast friends with the Black Sheep and his silver flask.

◆ The Nice Guy rips his hoodie on a random nail, and you can't wait to tear it off him.

◆ The Nice Guy nods at the bum who talks to himself, and you hang back to dispense advice.

◆ The Nice Guy downloads your favorite Smiths tracks but forgets to label the disk. Are those coaster rings on the CD? You pounce on him immediately.

Option 2: Think with Your Heart

So what would stop you from having an anonymous tryst with a sexy miscreant who wouldn't know a Talbots if he crashed his bike into one? Bad Boys consider casual freak-outs a dating norm. But you know in your growing heart that a Nice Guy isn't built to understand, or easily forgive, sexually erratic behavior. He's more stable, gentle, and trustworthy than that. Oh, stop your gagging. These are some of the reasons you fell for him . . . remember?

No doubt, back-to-back moments of couple-hood can nudge your better instincts to tumble like a row of dominos—and it only takes one Rob Reiner movie to start a chain of bad judgment calls. But here's the relief: You don't have to love every last minute spent in the Nice Guy's world. You do, however, have to care enough about your Nice Guy to stop yourself from defaulting to Emergency Action when you're feeling stifled, uncomfortable, or anxious. The Nice Guy would never pull a dirty move with a trailer park bimbo after QT with your obnoxious family. You owe him the same respect.

Now this isn't to say you won't need to decompress after an intense weekend together, because you will—and your feelings are completely legit. You may even need to remind yourself of who you are and think about what you loved doing before you began swapping recipes with your Nice Guy's mother. I should hope your interests weren't solely limited to sucking the faces off Bad Boys after too much hard liquor. And if they were, well, think harder.

Want to try an activity? No, you don't have to write anything down. Just stop your spinning head for a minute to remember at least five fun, seductive, or silly things you enjoy that have helped define you as a person. Recall the stuff you like to do alone, with friends, or on a date. If solo gallery hopping or attending film premieres with your guy friends is important and familiar

"My boyfriend gets up before I do every morning for work. Before he goes, he always leaves me a love note on a yellow Post-it. I've filled two shoeboxes with them."
—Sara, 27

(continued)

THIS MESSAGE BROUGHT TO YOU BY YOUR LOCAL SPONSOR

Falling off the wagon may seem like a blast until you wake with an uh-oh hangover and mysterious bruises. But if you ring your Sponsor as an alternative to a raucous romp, you won't have to battle dangerous impulses—because she'll be there to do it with you. (That is, after she confiscates your phone; no text messaging under the table!) What to do with your free time and anxious energy? Beyond the obvious movie or dinner plans, here are a few satisfying alternatives that will make it as good for her as it is for you.

BORROW A DOG

If you don't have your own canine, let someone else's lick you from head to toe. There's something to be said for doting love and attention—black Lab style.

INDULGE A VICE

Surely, Bad Boys aren't your only downfall. Smoke, drink, or eat too much ice cream with your Sponsor. Dating yucky men isn't as tempting in a smelly, bloated stupor.

PAINT A SONG

Spin vinyl that reflects your energy, while pushing oil paint across a canvas. Paint your self, Sponsor, or mood to visually record a head-space you don't want to visit again.

RETRO-SPEED WALK

It's so '80s, but fast-paced walking burns calories and increases endorphins. Incessant talking, insane gesturing, and furious arm waving shakes frustrations.

TALK TO A CHILD

Invite a toddler over to play. The child's innocence and need for attention will distract you from your libido. You'll feel great in the company of someone more helpless and less jaded than you.

THROW A SPA PARTY

Light candles, run a bath, pour a glass of wine, and loofah your body—while you call each other from different bathtubs in the same house (you get the land line). Once you prune, throw on sweats and watch a movie without having to spend a minute of time alone.

to you, make sure you haven't neglected these plans and people when coupling with a Nice Guy who has other interests. You've lost your self with Bad Boys before, and you quickly learned to regret it. Why make the same mistake with a Nice Guy who wouldn't expect this of you in the first place? Again, that's part of his charm. . . .

 WARNING: It's not until you're actually smack in the middle of a cutesy couple moment that your love life's wake-up call rings loud and clear.

Finally, make a plan to revisit three of your five activities before the week's end. I promise that the quick, condensed refresher will do wonders. So will drinking a bottle of bubbly, dancing in very high heels, and making out with your Nice Guy in a dimly lit lounge. The point is that acting young, dramatic, and independent shouldn't stop the moment you pair up. Managing your Nice Guy relationship is just a matter of breathing deeply, adjusting expectations, and creating a polite exit strategy the next time you anticipate a shaky situation. Just remember to wear a proper bra.

Chapter 9

En·List Your Guilty Conscience

STEP #8: Make a list of men, women, and supermodels you hurt as a Bad Boy Addickt and mentally prep to deal with every last one.

You're no angel. But once you acknowledge those you've harmed as a BBA, you'll be well on your way to shaking that devilish side that turned all the wrong heads. In order to do so, you must be willing to exhaust your mental energy and fancy handwriting skills in the name of recovery and peace of mind.

Block out a good portion of the weekend for this exercise. Though you don't have to abandon cocktail hour or the Sunday paper, you'll want to let this topic surface and settle and surface again—for at least 72 hours before you move on to the next, proactive step.

Everything Looks Better on Paper?

During the weekend, reflect on individuals you may have harmed as an addickt. These faces might include ditched Nice Guys, girlfriends, sisters, parents, neighbors, and even small dogs. Remember when you spread syphilis rumors about your Bad Boy ex's new girlfriend? She counts. And the time you kicked a neighbor's newly potted mums because your non-boyfriend boyfriend cancelled dinner at the last minute? The neighbor counts too. Begin with the usual suspects whose lives you may have directly damaged (family, friends), move to the tangential (their family and friends), and conclude with the circumstantial (innocent bystanders like waitresses and teacup Chihuahuas).

Next, settle into your favorite overstuffed chair and dim your overhead light so the following is soft on your eyes. List all names of those you've hurt on a sheet of paper, using stimulus throughout the weekend to help trigger surnames and memories. Who knows? Perfume counter attendants, op-eds about international politics, or guests at your boss's birthday party could spark spontaneous recollections. Tuck the list into your Balenciaga bag and carry it everywhere you go. Practically, the paper will be available for last-minute additions; metaphorically, the names will be with you at all times and weigh on your conscience like an unsettling pregnancy test.

 WARNING: Each name, number, and memory will undoubtedly elicit a flood of feelings that tear through your heart, mind, and spirit.

Finally, reshuffle your BBA victims in the order of those whose lives you trampled most to those you barely touched at all. Flip through black books and yellow pages to locate their phone numbers—and jot them next to corresponding names. In short form, list how your BBA antics potentially affected each person and what you'd say to them if given five minutes to make amends. These thoughts should fall under the umbrella of forgiveness and sympathy.

FORGET-YOU-NOTS

Unfortunately, BBAs don't just damage themselves. Others can be hurt by your behavior—and those who are most unexpectedly linked to your past are often the ones who can't shake the effect you had on them or someone they care about. You know your dear Mom, a devoted best friend, or an ex's long-suffering girlfriend are the most receptive to given apologies. But what about when you let a Bad Boy insult Dad or harass your dry cleaner? Or that time you assaulted a cop on his behalf? Here, a few reminders of those who may have been stuck in the midst of a Bad Boy debacle—and could easily slip your mind when drafting your forgiveness list.

CLEANING WOMAN

She forced you to haul your lazy tush off the divan after a dreadful breakup—if just to change the sheets.

THAT KID WITH A BLUE BALLOON

No matter how satisfying the pop, puncturing an otherwise cheery toy that belonged to a young stranger was just plain wrong. Especially on his birthday.

LANDLORD

You can only hang so many pictures over the holes you punched in his walls.

MANICURIST

She was a master at polishing chewed-down nail stubs after worrisome weekends. You should be ashamed that you under-tipped. . . .

NEIMAN'S SALESPERSON

Who cares if she gave that supermodel a discount on the perfect Chanel bag? You didn't need to get her fired just because the model is also your ex's screensaver.

NEW GIRLFRIEND'S MOM

A prank call is one thing. But did you have to compare her daughter's flowing locks to the vicious entanglement of snakes worn by Medusa?

4TH STREET

Littering an entire block with your Bad Boy's left-behinds is illegal, you know.

You'd Better Stock Up on Notepads for This One

Nowhere on your victim list should there be the name of a Bad Boy ex, whom you suspect is limping about with a damaged and crippled soul—compliments of your dumping savvy. Why the cold shoulder? Because Bad Boys have a special knack for making BBAs believe they're responsible for negative turns in their depressed, angst-ridden, and all around ruffian lifestyle. They may never have blamed you outright, but I doubt you weathered a stormy relationship without implied fault—especially since so few Bad Boys take responsibility for their dirty deeds.

It's Nice Guys who know that actions have consequences, and those consequences are attached to people with feelings. And as a recovering BBA, you know this too. So what kind of list should you make for all the Bad Boys you've (oh, admit it) loved before?

 WARNING: BBAs don't just damage themselves. Those who are most unexpectedly linked to your past are often the ones who can't shake the effect you had on them or someone they care about.

Though you might be tempted to catalog all the hearts that have broken yours and use it as your dog's pooper scooper, this will only feed your anger and sadness—which leaves no room for warm, loving gestures to those who deserve them. Instead, scribble the names of men who've upset you, and mentally forgive them for the confusion and angst they've caused. If you're feeling nostalgic, try this in a meditative posture while piping

Yanni through your iPod. More livid than melancholy? P.J. Harvey, a vat of Kettle One, and a box of Kleenex might be your best companions.

Either way, trudge down memory lane alone and loiter in the uncomfortable and often ickier than icky moments. Some of life's most important experiences can be the most painful. And sometimes you have to linger there before you can journey on.

Another reason you're to stay away from exes: This is not a time to search for explanations, recompense, or forgiveness. They moved on shortly after you walked out of their lives—and though they've stomped all over your being certainly doesn't mean you've left any imprint on theirs. Reconnecting with Bad Boys will only make you look pathetic or anxious to re-establish contact, neither of which is positive—or true, for that matter.

It's necessary for your own sake (not theirs!) to absolve louses of their misconduct, but never give them the satisfaction of knowing you did. Forget that whole "hate the sin, love the sinner" adage. Bad Boys aren't worth one valve of your heart that, when you were hanging out, beat to the pentameter of "Oh shit. Oh shit. Oh shit."

BBA recovery is about confronting all demons, but only battling those that are worth your energy.

"I had a boyfriend in high school who lived thirty minutes away from me. During the summer, I'd get home from work to find an iced coffee and muffin on my doorstep. He used to drive the entire way just to leave it for me." —Alyson, 25

Maybe Santa Was on to Something . . .

Making a list to organize your thoughts and feelings is as much about practicality as it is about catharsis. The process of considering, recording, editing, and then reconsidering your deeds on paper will free your brain to focus on maintaining other elements of recovery that we've discussed in previous chapters. You'll also have more headspace to devote to personal wellness. (Remember the simple joys and benefits of afternoon walks, Chinese acupuncture, and long-distance phone rants? Don't abandon them simply because you're on a guided path.) By putting pen to paper, you'll literally release years of BBA tension that have caused you frustration, remorse, and resentment—not to mention, a handful of friends exhausted by your drama.

Each name, number, and memory will undoubtedly elicit a flood of feelings that tear through your heart, mind, and spirit before they ultimately find a home on your notepad. Expect to cry, laugh, shudder in recognition, or scream with utter surprise as you record each one. Share these emotions with your Sponsor, a trusted friend, your Higher Power, or even your journal. You've already spent years getting in the way of your own happiness; don't regress now by sinking yourself into emotional quicksand. It's time to look ahead to a more freeing future.

The energy you've expended, simply by holding on to the guilt you've stored for having wronged the undeserved, could easily power a small river yacht—with a roof deck for sunning. In fact, I wouldn't be surprised if your emotional discomfort has physically manifested itself over the years in the form of back pain, stomachaches, nausea, depression, or general fatigue. Stress lowers your immune system, and there's something to be said for a healthy mind, body, and spirit connection. I've always found that when my head and body aren't joyfully in sync, it's not long before I lose my voice or catch an inexplicable virus (and yes, I pop vitamins, eat well, and exercise regularly). If your mind is capable of storing stress, and your mind is part of your body . . . I have every reason to believe that guilt, angst, blame, and other emotional muck from your life will eventually settle in a physically unsettling way. You already have enough to worry about on the road to addicktive recovery. No need to battle a hacking cough or gray hairs, as well.

THIS IS THE ONLY TIME I'LL CONDONE BOTTLED FEELINGS

Don't get me wrong: I'm a huge fan of uncorking emotions. But because contacting a Bad Boy to explain how you feel will likely lead to frustration, regret, or a heady nightcap—which could ultimately set you back a few chapters in the 12-Step process—I'd be a sloppy advice giver if I didn't suggest a few options about what to do with the Bad Boy list once it's drafted.

Rather than burn, tear, or flush your Bad Boy inventory, empty a container or three of your favorite social lubricant (Chardonnay bottles work just as well as Diet Coke cans) with two good friends. Sip toward the bottom while slaying Bad Boy recollections. Once the vessel is empty, drop your list inside and ritualistically toss it into the nearest body of water—whether it's the Hudson River or the decorative koi pond next door. Your Higher Power will make sure it reaches an appropriate end. Perhaps the bottle will bump against a surfer girl's board and forewarn her about a man she's currently dating; or maybe the glass container will get stuck between two large rocks and crash to its destiny. Regardless, you've now relinquished these men from your life! You've sent them back into the unknown to achieve their due fate, even if that fate is a Staten Island landfill—which wouldn't be such an unfit end, come to think of it.

Sensibly speaking, constructing a list of those with whom you'd like to make amends is also a practical means to holding yourself accountable for the next step in our program. Whether you've made a grocery list for a special recipe or a chart of errands and chores in the past, I'm sure you're familiar with how helpful it is to organize scattered thoughts into tangible realities. Once you've paid for your milk, or in our case called your amendee, there's a huge satisfaction that comes with crossing a must-do off your list. Productivity will encourage you to move on to your next success, too.

In this chapter, you began the process of making amends through preparation and visualization. In the next section, you'll actually put those elements into practice. Compartmentalizing a thought, writing down its goal, managing the problem, and then mastering the challenge—in a planned, sequential order—can't help but yield a sense of accomplishment. The procedure is as much about satisfaction as it is about relief.

Chapter 10

Reach Out and Touch Someone (But Keep Your Hands to Yourself)

STEP #9: Make frank amends with those you hurt as a Bad Boy Addickt—unless doing so will damage them, others, or score you a restraining order.

Did you honestly think I'd ask you to make that handy little list of trampled lives without encouraging you to do something with it? You silly tart! You're going to use this record to redeem your wrongdoings for the good of others' psyches—and, just as important, for the good of yours.

Demanding Bad Boys often insisted you put their needs first; when the truth is, you should always focus on what it takes to qualify you and your happiness. Even when you're making amends with other people, you'll reap secondary benefits because it feels nice to do the right thing for others—especially when they express their appreciation, reciprocally. Plus, you'll be doing this over the phone which means you can save face should the need arise.

The exercise upon which you're about to embark is also fabulous practice for future Nice Guy encounters and personal growth, in general. It's a lesson in recognizing your wrongs, asking for forgiveness, accepting that some mistakes aren't pardonable, and learning from those that are. All of these actions require sincere objectives and open communication—two musts in any Nice Guy relationship. So consider this exercise as much about your past as it is about your future.

Making Amends: The Three Cs

There's a difference between merely contacting people on your list and actually connecting with them. Obviously, the second has a deeper impact on how you affect others' lives and how much time and heart you devote to each apology. Connections are something for which you should *selectively* strive as you reach out to BBA-exploit victims. Don't waste connection energy on apologizing to gas station attendants who doled out discount oil checks in exchange for flirtatious ego boosts; if you feel compelled to apologize to someone like this, such an amendee would fall under the contact category. I'd even limit your connection apologies to six and your contact apologies to four to avoid emotional exhaustion. Extend this exercise over a two-week period so your words don't sound like a scratched and skipping self-help CD—and if you're on a roll, draw the line at two per day. Repetition dulls your apology's impact on its listener, especially if your delivery becomes robotic or watered down. Moreover, you don't need to remind *yourself* on an hourly basis how your BBA-ness made others sour. Your goal is to feel refreshed when you've finished each call, not further deflated or self-doubting.

Which is why you'll make contacts and connections, but deliberately avoid collisions. Collisions are the personal catastrophes for which you were a catalyst—scenarios that landed victims in therapy, caused them to avoid entire neighborhoods for fear of a run-in, or rock silently in the corner of a room,

"Without being asked, my husband does dozens of small things every day to make our home run more smoothly. As I say this, I hear him emptying the dishwasher and starting dinner. He's also watching our son at the same time." —Amy, 27

unable to digest solid foods. To run with the car metaphor, collisions can be head-on smash fests between you and another. I've even caused a few bumper-to-bumper pile-ups myself, in which I've wronged a person directly, who then upset someone else, who then spurned a total stranger . . . and so on.

The most disastrous occurred when a mutual friend fixed me up with her guy's best friend, who happened to be a Bad Boy. He also happened to be dating another woman—while I was occasionally making out with another man. The messy scenario came to a crashing halt when our friend heard a rumor about the rampant romps and put an end to the chaos. This led to trampled self-esteem, lost friendships, blocked phone calls, tearful apologies, and far too many details to sensibly collate. As you can imagine, trying to contact everyone involved in this collision would have been an impossibly moot point—and a major time eater. Knowing my luck, I'd have spent two weeks simply trying to get everyone on the phone, and then failing miserably because nobody would have taken my calls.

What's more, by the time you're ready to make amends, it's quite likely that victims of truly extreme, destructive collisions have already taken action to mend their emotional boo-boos. No need to rub sea salt into the open wound. Plus, there's always the chance that offering an apology will sound self-serving—and in a way it is (flashback: Remember when Carrie offered an apology to Mr. Big's soon-to-be ex-wife for sleeping with him on *Sex and the City*? Imagine that scenario in your own life, minus Carrie's trashy newsprint dress). Our goal is for you to overcome your BBA habits, and asking for forgiveness is intended to provide an "aah" moment as each person listens to your apology and hopefully admires your chutzpah for confronting them. In addition to accolades, you should also expect them to tell you how much you sucked (past tense) and why. You've never given your victims a forum to speak, and now that you are, it's unrealistic to think they'll simply curtsy and move on. They've been harboring as much confusion as you have—but this scenario will help you iron out differences and find a better headspace together.

Which reminds me: Not all candid apologies will awaken friendships and usher in fruit baskets. Some contact and connection efforts might lead to hang-ups or vengeful tirades—complete with profanity, nicknames, and death threats. If this happens, don't take it personally, and simply drop to the next name on your list. Replace Angry Person with another from your past, and cross your fingers for better luck this time. If you hear frustration in people's voices, don't interpret it as criticism but as a way that that person is expressing something they need from you (you left them with baggage; they may want to drop it at your door). If your victim attacks or name-calls, do not reciprocate. In a way, you're giving the gift of regret and sincerity; once you've handed it over, it's the recipient's choice as to whether he/she wants to save the ribbon or use it as a noose.

It's What You Say *and* How You Say It

When doling out sentiments like a Hallmark exec, there's no concrete way to say how you feel so it resonates with your listener and reaps emotional gratification for you too. But there are a few basics to which you might want to stick.

When you work the digits, remember that the person on the receiving end is 1) not expecting your call; and 2) has no idea how much you've grown since you were an opportunistic BBA. Jot down two specific talking points and one joke in case you totally blank out. Overlook the shock or appall in their voices, and immediately explain why you're calling. Be specific. Apologize for the way you acted as a BBA, and reassure them you're not calling because you need something but because you'd like to say you're sorry for the role you've played in their life.

 WARNING: Not all candid apologies will awaken friendships and usher in fruit baskets. Some might lead to hang-ups or vengeful tirades—complete with profanity, nicknames, and death threats.

Your goal is not to gain new friendships from this exercise—though that may be an eventual outcome. In some cases, you'll repair relationships, and in others, you'll simply apologize. Compliment and thank the person often: for what they meant to you in the past, and what they think of you now—even if it is that you're a big, fat loser. Stock phrases like "I'm sorry I hurt you, but I'm working hard to stop licking caramel off someone else's boyfriend now that I'm in recovery" or "I've always loved your honesty, even if I used it against you as a BBA" say you care and are making a well-intentioned effort to change hurtful behavior. If you speak from an honest place, then nothing you say can be wrong because it's how you feel. It also helps to keep chitchat brief, because once you start to babble on and on about the hows and whys and wheres of an apology, you might never shut up. Don't dig yourself a deeper hole than when you began.

Just as important as what you say during your monologue, is how you say it. Especially since you'll be making amends over the phone (no wimpy e-mails or bold in-person talks allowed), your voice's tone is the equivalent of body language and facial contortions. Sounding either too chipper or morose sends a message that you're an easily aroused extremist—which you are, but this is not the time to express it. Keep your voice even but not monotone; shoot for a few octaves above a whisper to express remorse without evoking pity. Do not gasp, whimper, or sigh. Do not allow for lulls, and if there is an awkward silence, avoid breathing heavily into the phone like an asthmatic. Do not interrupt when the other person is talking—and that includes chewing, coughing, or sniffling. Active listeners do not engage in bodily functions.

With a tissue box to your right and a vocal lubricant to your left (I prefer soymilk, myself), indulge in cathartic remorse after you toss the

"I'm English, and I miss Bonfire Night on November 5th. My Nice Guy came to my apartment with a huge saucepan, a bunch of twigs, and broken branches. He took them out onto my tiny NYC balcony and made me a fire. Brilliant!"—Sarah, 32

receiver. There's plenty of time for drama when you're not try-ing to be the embodiment of composure to people who think you're already a mess to begin with.

> **WARNING:** You'll be tempted to share the outcomes of these conversations with your clan, which could lead to belittling the situation or distorting the experience for the sake of a good story.

Composure Is Like Yoga for Your Conscience

When confessing wrongs, it's important to maintain an air of composure so you can focus, breathe properly, and avoid lower-back pain when hunched over the phone.

Before each call, be sure to align your posture so you're in a comfortable, appropriate position as you spill your gizzard to someone who thinks you're a no-good emotional scamp. If this tip doesn't yield sufficient solace, give these other suggestions a whirl.

◆ Put a comfort song softly on repeat to soothe your weary nerves. For obvious reasons, "What a Wonderful World" by Louis Armstrong works better than "Easy to Be Stu-pid" by Howlin' Maggie.

◆ Settle into a cushioned seat that surrounds you with feathered hospitality—or allows for a self-deprecating sink if the call goes awry.

◆ Light a scented candle, *if* you can resist playing with can-dle wax during the call. Focus! Focus! Focus!

◆ Unbutton the top clasp of your jeans and close your eyes. Breathe in for three counts, and hold your breath while imagining a blank slate on which no chalky judgment inhibits thoughts or actions. Exhale for three counts and smile.

Let Go, and Let Girlfriends . . .

Right about now would be a great time for you to hang with your closest, warmest, most forgiving, and outright hilarious girlfriends. During these two weeks, you'll hear about a past you'd rather forget—and be told that your actions hurt more than an elbow to premenstrual boobs. That's a heavy load for any person to carry, much less a recovering BBA. To balance the impact of the make-amends exercise with unconditional love, find time to chill with girlfriends who care about you when you're at your best and your worst. Unless you really need an adoring Sponsor in tow, I suggest you leave her behind so you can remember that being an addickt is only part of your person—and not your entire identity.

The plan? Indulge in four outings over the two-week amends period, but please do not couple them with emotionally draining, make-amends phone calls. You'll be tempted to share the outcomes of these conversations with your clan, which could lead to belittling the situation or distorting the experience for the sake of a good story. Instead, spend some time alone after each call to help you process and better learn from your experience to enforce a bit of clarity.

Finally, save these easy-breezy experiences for days off, and think of them as rewards for personal growth—not as an easy escape from responsibility or reality. I shouldn't have to say it, but I'll err on the side of safety: This means no BBA indulgences with your friends, no matter how tempting. Girl time isn't a free pass to fall off the wagon; it's an opportunity to celebrate your beautiful evolution. Here, a few suggestions on how to make the most of it.

◆ **Very often, upscale hotels offer afternoon tea and house beautiful spas.** Book a hot-coal massage for yourself, as two friends receive their treatments of choice. Once everyone's relaxed, rejuvenated, and dabbed with lavender oil, saunter up to the tea room for champagne and sweets!

◆ **Free your mind . . . and your friends will follow.** Make an appointment with a well-respected hypnotist in town—but do your research first to find a reputable talent. While under his spell, hypnotists have the power to encourage your subconscious to help beat smoking habits, make career changes, improve family dynamics, boost exercise regimes—or even stick to stabilizing recovery programs. Don't buy the hocus pocus? Ask the hypnotist if you can stay in the room, as each of your friends is put into a trance. You'll be instantly convinced. But no giggling allowed. . . .

◆ **Rent bikes with fellow cycling novices and explore a neighboring town on wheels!** The exercise will invigorate, and you'll have a sure laugh (with or at each other is debatable) when you're forced to push the damn thing uphill. Buy wicker baskets for your friends, fill with fresh flowers, and attach to each bike. Dole out arrangements to little girls in pretty dresses, en route.

◆ **Take a road trip.** Start early, sing to a mix tape, stop for a picnic lunch—and drive until you reach an interesting unknown. Just don't plan your destination! The best antique shops, ice cream stands, drive-in theaters, and small-town boutiques are often accidental finds.

◆ **Make a reading date.** Invite lit lovers to your house with their favorite books, light candles, and provide plenty of munchies, wine, and blankets to go around. Read favorite passages as you stumble upon them—or keep quiet for the night. Curling up with a good book and good friends is the perfect balance between alone time and girl time. Slumber party, optional.

Chapter 11

From Your Mouth to Everyone Else's Ears

STEP #10: Continue to check in with your Addickt conscience—and when you screw up, don't be such an exhausting wimp. Admit it, already. . . .

Though you may feel like you've already taken more inventory than the stock boy at Piggly Wiggly, recovering BBAs need to continue to personally assess their behavior because we've been known to regress into unmanageable territory. You've broken a serious sweat acknowledging flaws and moving past them. And with so much work under your Hermès belt, why not pay attention to upkeep?

You wouldn't spend thousands on your new duvet—and then allow small, irritable children in dirty old sneakers to jump on your high thread count. A healthy love life is more impressive than crisp Frette linens, so treat it with the respect and coddling it deserves.

The more self-aware you become, the easier it will be to recognize your weaknesses—which makes them easier to battle and eventually stamp out of your psyche, once and for all. On trickier days, I can't think of anything more difficult to resist than an untamable Bad Boy—except maybe, an untamable Bad Boy wielding a box of Baci chocolates. Though your

Sponsor should continue to keep tabs and receive updates on your whereabouts, it's primarily a recovering BBA's responsibility to know doable from ditchable men. Years after you've outgrown your Bad Boy phase and this trusty guide is peppered with dust and fingerprints, you'll still collide with precarious situations that require conscious decision-making—and a quieting of naturally reckless instincts.

At that point, the best thing to do is simply admit when you're weak, you're wrong, and you're randy . . . and then confess it to a trusted source. Again: Your Sponsor, Higher Power, therapist, or mirrored reflection will all do the trick. Acknowledging weakness can be the real proof of success, not how often you resist temptation. The process of saying "I really blow," and knowing what that means, often proves that you've recognized and assessed your BBA thought or deed—which is more than you can say than when you began this process.

Check-Ins That Don't Require a Second Key

To check in with your BBA conscience is to take personal stock of your progress. This includes how well you've shed your addicktive skin, whether your Nice Guy relationships are satisfying, ways in which recovery has changed your social life—and any other BBA notion that paints your identity. There was a time when you used to look forward to out-of-town guests that left a disheveled imprint behind, when the words "check in" meant you played a Bad Boy's Mrs. at a shmancy hotel with an extra key to the minibar. But with that privilege came a sinking, hollow suspicion that you were as disposable as his free mini bottles of Kiehl's products and the $25 bagel plate from room service. Bad Boys always left you a breathless shell of a woman. But how often was that a positive thing?

I'll agree that there's an ease and familiar relief that comes with allowing life to be messy, as you wade through the clutter to make sense of it all. But as a recovering BBA, you're armed with self-knowledge and decisiveness. You're in the habit of making thought-out choices to avoid a chaotic cleanup before disaster strikes. And though it's a bit more work, I promise that forethought's emotional payoff will be better than any surprise visitor you've ever had.

 WARNING: A reformed BBA will reel in a gaggle of Nice Guys whether she likes the attention or . . . who am I kidding? Of course she'll like the attention!

From now on, the term "check in" will assume an entirely different meaning. Twice a month, run with your stream of consciousness either on paper or aloud. Use reflective moments to think about the past two weeks—and note when you mentally connect and check out of conversations, meetings, movies, etc. Slowly but surely, you'll realize how often Nice Guy moments are an ingredient to long-term happiness—even if they take the shape of clients, friends, or the local butcher. Gather info on a regular basis, and then use it to make proactive decisions about the people and places that make you feel your best. Gradually, your well-trained instincts will act as burly bodyguards to your heart and you'll instinctively avoid BBA situations. You'll also understand and adjust nuances of behavior: For example, when you're slipping or when you're acting out, you'll know how to shift your attitude accordingly.

The more you take inventory, the less laborious it feels. Your composition book becomes your friend, emotive speak becomes intuitive, and the Nice Guys in your life ease into your routine more gracefully. And when you finally achieve balance, playing Mrs. at a shmancy hotel with a Nice Guy will be twice as kinky because you'll finally act like the person you were meant to be.

Come Again?

Okay, here's the weirdest part about being a recovering BBA. At one time, Bad Boys swarmed to my side; whether they fell into needy, selfish, commitment-phobic, or emotionally warped categories no longer feels relevant. Perhaps I knew just what to say or how to dress or which wingmen would help bring them back for more. But since I've been with my Nice Guy, I swear on my boyfriend's tender kisses that any admirers I've had since are also classifiably Nice. In fact, I haven't turned the head of a Bad Boy in over three years! It's not that I've lost my edge— and unless they're well-practiced liars, friends tell me I'm not a dog's lunch. So what gives?

I think the trick is that I've simply rid my immediate circle of Bad Boys, so now outsiders are no longer drawn to me. I must not emit the scent of a girly girl looking for lust, but that of

"On my birthday, this delicious hipster-type bought me the most expensive shot at the bar: a Louis XIII. It cost him $130!"—Elisabeth, 32

a woman who trusts the power of real love. And while apathy toward a typical letch might have attracted bogus men in the past, it hasn't done a thing for me lately. Perhaps because I'm no longer manufacturing indifference to entice them, my who-gives-a-shit attitude is actually earnest—and something tells me that Bad Boys can sense it.

This isn't to say I've had fewer secret admirers than I did as an active BBA. And neither will your foxy self. Even if you're dating someone, Nice Guys are still guys—and men will always be attracted to what they can't have, no matter how pure their hearts. But because your values, habits, and social circles have been tweaked, your stock has risen. Now you'll attract men who are as drawn to your presence as they are to your exposed clavicle. In fact, you'll find yourself starting to ignore Bad Boy advances and shutting them out of conversation as quickly as you did a Nice Guy before you began this program. The difference is, you won't even realize it's happening. So if taking inventory and admitting mistakes helps you continue to be the best you can be, and effortlessly introduces you to great men, then tossing your BBA rep will be a welcome change!

The Nice Guy Catch: When There's More Than One

As I mentioned, a reformed BBA will reel in a gaggle of Nice Guys whether she likes the attention or . . . who am I kidding? Of course she'll like the attention! Just keep in mind, a Nice Guy's MO will be much less overt than a Bad Boy's, and sometimes accidental. My reformed BBA friend Nikki has a wonderful Nice Guy boyfriend, and his Nice Guy competition managed to slip past her radar because the two were friends for months before their feelings took a turn for the romantic. The friendship was intimate and intense, as Nikki and Nice Guy #2 spent valuable time together while exploring mutual interests: cooking, long runs, dog walks, etc. Unlike Nikki's Bad Boy exes, her Nice Guy boyfriend exhibited no jealousy because he genuinely trusted their relationship. And choosing between the two men was a huge mental and emotional fiasco since, unlike her Bad Boy exes, neither man was obviously unworthy and both were highly susceptible to being hurt. Uncharacteristically, Nikki found herself hoping that one guy would call her a fat aardvark, curse at a lazy-eyed waiter, or make a pass at her prim sister—just to make the decision process easier. But after taking *lots* of inventory, Nikki realized her loving beau was The One—and the Nice Guy friend eventually understood because he wanted the best for her.

 WARNING: Though your Sponsor should continue to keep tabs and receive updates on your whereabouts, it's primarily a recovering BBA's responsibility to know doable from ditchable men.

After chatting to oodles of reformed BBAs, I learned that the details of Nikki's predicament aren't uncommon, although it's also not a given that Nice Guy love triangles wrap up so neatly. You're dealing with earnest emotions here, and earnest heartache is a reality. So while that flirty BBA nature might be used to engage multiple interests at one time, remember that you're now playing with a new archetype. Adjust your vixen affinities for everyone's sake. Spend time with as many Nice Guys as you'd like, but be forewarned that the sticky catch with caring about so many good boys is that, well, they're good boys who really are worth caring about.

Chapter 12

Familiar Tales of Whoa

STEP #11: Through meditation and support from the Addickt community, keep boosting your dating acumen. Couple your will with that of others to learn from their stories and mimic their careful and conscientious prowess.

During any 12-step program, you'd be forced to sit through open meetings and spill your addicted guts to strangers. If that weren't difficult enough, you'd then convene with people who eat stale donuts and drink even staler coffee with powdered cream after they've gone all weepy. Since this isn't any 12-step program, I instead hope you're slouching in that overstuffed chair with your puggle, Lolita, while nibbling strawberries with powdered sugar and feeling increasingly empowered. Because that's the kind of 12-Stepper you are.

However! In the name of voyeurism and a traditional dose of self-help, I asked five women at different stages in their BBA recovery to share their stories as if a day-old éclair depended on it. And wouldn't you know, these women were thrilled to tell their anecdotes. Not that I'm shocked: BBAs, recovered or not, are more likely to be lip-locked than tight-lipped anyway.

Since Nice Guy sobriety can also be maintained at group meetings, you may find that reading the following stories satiates your tell-all needs. Then again, they might also prove so inspiring that you'll rush to start your own biweekly sharing group, perhaps in the form of dinner parties or gourmet coffee klatches. If so, then God bless.

Gabrielle
The Tease

I live in L.A., and Hollywood is the land of ambitious Bad Boys with self-serving careers and self-made identities—and I'm trying very hard not to love it so much. Nobody moves here to make the world a better place, so most men date their jobs when they're not dating a woman who doesn't demand too much time or energy. I used to tell myself that L.A. men weren't up to the task of dating me until I realized that Bad Boys aren't up to the task of dating anyone who's not made of cardboard.

Who's on my Bad Boy resume? There's The Director, The Editor . . . so few are assigned real names until they earn them, and unfortunately I only tend to date above the line so I can IMDB their profiles. (It's much more efficient than Google.) I don't have a gold digger mentality, but I am seduced by a successful Hollywood Bad Boy's lifestyle: the cars, the houses, the artwork. Sometimes my calls are returned, sometimes they aren't. I tell myself, "Oh, he's cutting or he's shooting," when one minute I have dinner plans, and the next I don't. But that's just how things are here.

The problem is that I'm never sure if these guys haven't called in a month because they're with someone else, or not interested, or on location. I don't want to be Drama Girl and pitch a fit. I want these guys to know I'm spontaneous, flexible, and easy.

I used to think I could match their games—and that I'm the real tease. But I'm starting to think I'm only teasing myself.

When The Director calls for dinner, for example, he makes a ticking noise on the phone and says, "Hear that? It's the Chance Machine. You have a chance to have dinner with me tonight, and it's waiting for your answer. . . . " I'm not going to tell him I'm already in my pajamas, with my teeth brushed, and my dog fed, reading *Shopgirl* for the tenth time. Usually, I give men until 11:20 P.M. to ask me out, and I don't expect to hear from them any earlier. We watch movies, fool around, and call it a date. Or at least I do.

Recently, though, I've worked hard to turn a new corner. Kicking a Bad Boy habit is like riding an unruly horse: When you've been bucked off so many times, it really starts to hurt and is no longer fun. Now, I'm spending a lot of time with a Nice Guy who's supportive and accommodating. I don't know if my Nice Guy relationship will have a Hollywood ending, but I do feel I'm on the road to recovery.

Ava
The Caretaker

I dated Peter for eight years—during much of which, he screwed around on me. I pretended not to know about his Bad Boy phi-landering because he managed to counterbalance his cheating heart with a very smooth exterior: We spent anniversaries at B&Bs, and once he assembled a book of memories and photos that reflected our whole relationship. I was close to his family, he was always demonstrative of his affections—and it wasn't until a tall blonde stranger told me she'd spent the better part of the last year with him that something in me snapped.

That's when I finally dumped him.

It wasn't a clean break with Peter, however—and we recycled our relationship at least five times over two years. I told myself he was young, cheating was a phase, and that he was a damaged soul in need of rescue. That was a dynamic that repeatedly played out during our time together: He'd feel hurt, I'd play Florence Nightingale; his family didn't love him; he hated himself; he was so misunderstood. . . . You know the drill.

Months later, I rebounded with the nicest guy named Matt. He was a law student during the year and a waiter at my parents' golf club during the summers. Matt splurged on expensive jewelry, spent quality time with my dad on the course . . . but my body just couldn't give in to his touch. I didn't feel the pull that I had with Peter, regardless of whether Matt was a Nice Guy. But I really wanted to like him—and he was so instrumental in helping me get through my breakup that we lasted an entire year before I called it quits.

I'm not sorry I dumped Matt, because he opened me up to another kind of man—one who's gentle, faithful, honest, calls often, and has female friends he hasn't slept with. In a way, he acted as training wheels for me because the next Nice Guy I fell for is one that I've been

"My Nice Guy and I don't celebrate Valentine's Day, because he says that every day is Valentine's Day. I get chocolates, massages, and surprises on a regular basis—and we've been together for two years." —Sue, 19

with for three years and counting. He's generous, doting, and all-around worthy.

That's the trick with dating a Nice Guy: You can't expect immediate va-va-voom. They're available. They remember your name. They want relationships. You have to open yourself up to their charm, and then wait. Wait for their value to register with your mind, and for your mind to accept and then process a new brand of courtship that's unlike anything you've ever experienced. When you date a Bad Boy, you have to be patient with him. When you date a Nice Guy, you must be patient with yourself.

 WARNING: When you date a Bad Boy, you have to be patient with him. When you date a Nice Guy, you must be patient with yourself.

The Comparison Shopper

I spent the weekend with my family in Connecticut and brought this guy Mark, strictly as a friend. Mark's the quintessential Nice Guy: He gave my mother wine as a hostess gift, treated us to dinner, and couldn't keep a compliment to himself. I was too distracted to care because on Sunday night, I planned to meet for a hot rendezvous with Duncan, an aloof Bad Boy who'd cancelled our three previous dates. He asked to meet at a smoky, dark bar around 6 P.M.—and this time, I thought he'd make it. I'd snogged mystery men before, but Duncan wooed me with so many flirty nicknames and like-minded allusions that I never thought he'd break my heart as often as he did our plans.

On Sunday night, 6 P.M. rolled around . . . then 6:15 P.M., then 6:30—at which point, I asked the bartender, "So how long should I wait for a man before I can actually say I've been stood up?" The bartender feigned surprise, as did fellow patrons. "You were what?" asked a tall smug-married who overheard the conversation. The bartender elbowed in: "Who is this guy? I'll take you out!" The scene was straight from a bad romantic comedy with a mortifying second act. I walked home alone, wishing I'd spent the night with Mark. I missed him.

Yet just before he dropped me off for my non-date, Mark said we couldn't talk for a few days. He was hurt because I told him I couldn't reciprocate his romantic feelings, and now the brief but meaningful loss made me feel sick and dizzy. The three sangrias I drank while waiting for Duncan didn't help.

But as most Nice Guys do, Mark came around. He called two days later and asked me to the U.S. Open since we're both tennis fanatics. (Meanwhile, Duncan e-mailed a lame apology, which I ignored.) I don't know if it was our box seats or the roar of the crowd, but my hormones swung into full gear. I leaned over and thanked Mark for the night with a big old kiss—and my 5'4" man suddenly grew four inches.

I was drawn to Mark because we had so much fun, and he made it abundantly and sincerely clear that he was attracted to me—a refreshing change from Bad Boy garbage. Thanks to my past, I thought I'd end up with an unavailable, towering hunka-hunka man boy; dating was always about the chase. But with Mark, he actually wanted to talk, take me to dinner, and spring for weekends in Napa Valley. Our courtship felt too easy at first—but once I relaxed into it, I realized Mark loved qualities about me which most Bad Boy studs find goofy: my sense of humor, my low tolerance for strong liquor. That's the best thing about Mark, though: We can be silly together—and although we've dated for five months, it wasn't until three days ago that I reached holy-shit mode. It's been a slow and steady climb but I'm still learning the Nice Guy ropes.

I recently saw Duncan at a holiday party, and though I might have otherwise gone out of my way to make us both feel cool and comfortable—I outright ignored him and stuck to Mark's side. That man is everything I deserve. And even if he's not The One, I know a Bad Boy will never be.

Mirabelle
The Timing Whiz

After I dumped my boyfriend of eight years (who was more "blah" than Good or Bad), I went on a Bad Boy spree. There was Ali, who fed me grapes and said he'd introduce me to Madonna; there was Jean Pierre, to whom I wrote a thank-you note after a one-night stand; and Marcus, who impregnated another woman while we dated for five months. I could go on, but I might sound like an international harlot. While on my cavorting spree, I met Alfonzo: an Italian Bad Boy with a deviant twinkle in his eye that spelled trouble, which only made me want him more. Alfonzo had serious game, but nothing I couldn't see through: For example, he took me to five restaurants where he thought he could impress me by introducing me to the managers for special treatment. Little did he know that I knew the joints were all owned by the same man. . . .

Alfonzo had major trust issues, and for over a month, we'd have quick but fabulous dinners and then book it back to his house for hours of unbelievable sex. He was like a drug. I'd heard of great chemistry, but I was very much addickted to Alfonzo's . . . everything. For him, I endured my first Brazilian bikini wax—and then let him generously smear me with Nutella. Between trysts, he also gave me brilliant tips about how to be a bitch in the business world, which I still use today. Alfonzo had a 30-day expiration date, though, and I gave him the ax when things started to feel really intense and a bit animalistic. I felt objectified, and I told him so. Of course, that didn't stop Alfonzo from asking me if I wanted one last go after we said our goodbyes.

Typical bastard.

Exactly 12 months passed before I saw Alfonzo again. And during our time apart, I realized that nobody compared to him in a lot of ways, and I wanted to connect on a deeper level. He also had a lot of growing up to do on his own. We kept in touch via e-mail and phone— as I strategically painted myself as the compassionate, driven, stable, and respectful woman he overlooked when our relationship was based only on groping, sweaty, casual sex. I knew these were core values he admired in a woman and that he'd want in a wife. Slowly, Alfonzo began to appreciate my business side and loyalty to family. I kept our talks short, sweet, and

"The nicest guy I ever dated flew from another country unannounced, three months after we broke up, so he could make a case for why we should still be together. It worked, and now we're engaged." —Carmella, 34

smart. When we finally met for a drink, it was our first real date—though we only went as friends. By the night's end, we were on each other's laps. And when I went home alone, I knew it was for real.

In a way, Alfonzo and I worked backward. We had sex before we were truly intimate. And I've never let him take me for granted since—and we've been married now for two years—because that's not the woman he fell in love with. Romances that start with fire, fury, and artificial passion do not a solid relationship make—at least not right away. Sometimes you have to relinquish control and let timing work in your favor. I couldn't have tamed or changed Alfonzo; and he couldn't have loved me before he was ready.

 WARNING: Romances that start with fire, fury, and artificial passion do not a solid relationship make—at least not right away. Sometimes you have to relinquish control and let timing work in your favor.

Olivia
The Makeover Artist

Since I have to count, I dated about eight Bad Boys in two years. (It sounds like a lot, but they don't stick around long.) I love their look and how they just smell like . . . life. I swear, if Calvin Klein could bottle that irresistible do-me-now essence, he'd make a mint. I've always been drawn to the usual suspects: Bad Boys who know what to say and how to say it. Then there's the whole sex thing. Nobody can manipulate, massage, and satisfy my senses like a Bad Boy can. Too bad I knew I had to run from the whole species when my last Bad Boy dumped me for a Playboy centerfold with plastic boobs. Does it get any more cliché than that?

I met my Nice Guy while having dinner with girlfriends at my neighborhood trattoria. My friend complained that the food was cold, and the owner—a tall, strong, manly man named Michael—offered his apologies and a complimentary Pinot. When I paid the check, we began to talk—but when he asked me out, I turned him down. Michael didn't seem like my type: He had a ponytail and vintage leather jacket, which he wore with tapered Levis. Anyway, a year later I went back to the restaurant and he sent over a cocktail napkin that said: "The bartender remembers you." I looked over and saw Michael working his bar—and I smiled back. We've been together for four years since.

Michael is obviously a Nice Guy—but boy, did he need a makeover! That's something everyone should know about Nice Guys: Their style is seldom impeccable, and when you're used to I'm-too-sexy-for-a-commitment Bad Boys, a Nice Guy's fashion issues can be hard on the eyes. But you have to look for potential. After Michael and I fell in love, I worked my magic: We bought him a pair of boots here, a new wool coat there. And I convinced him to chop the Fabio hair! That was the hardest part. I won't lie: It took a little sexual coercion. In any event, he now looks like the Bad Boys I adored but has the heart of a golden Good Boy. He's the perfect mix!

As most Nice Guys do, Michael also buys me flowers, is great to my friends, and his eyes never wander. But I knew this one was for me when my father died. His sympathy was so authentic that it hurt me to watch him suffer. Right after Dad passed,

I was at my mother's an hour from home—and just when I thought I couldn't take any more tears or remember-when stories, the doorbell rang. Two black Lincolns filled with food from Michael's restaurant arrived, still hot, with a beautiful letter addressed to my family expressing his regrets and naming all the wonderful memories he had of my father. I can't tell you how that affected me. A Bad Boy would never pull a move like that, not if his pot stash depended on it. I may have had to give Michael a makeover in the physical sense, but I wouldn't change a thing about my Nice Guy's emotional IQ.

Chapter 13

You're Not So Bad Yourself

STEP #12: Revel in your emotional, spiritual, and sexual awakening—and subtly spread the Bad Boy Addickt message to as many tartlets as you can.

You're almost there! You're on your 12th Step! It's almost time to celebrate—but not so fast. More than a few BBAs argue that this final step is actually the most important one to implement when kicking your habit. It's about recognizing The New You and talking her up to BBAs who could use a lesson (or 12). Every BBA can point to emotional calluses caused by too much Bad Boy friction—and that's a platform on which you can relate.

I'm not suggesting you bedazzle T-shirts, knock on doors with bright pamphlets, or shout your success from a rooftop terrace. But should you recognize a BBA in need, trust that it's your responsibility to reach out. Not in an overzealous evangelical way. Or in any solicitous or aggressive fashion reminiscent of telemarketers or the Haré Krishnas. Subtlety is of utmost importance here. As you fully realize your recovering BBA status, recall how you felt when you realized you first had a problem: Doubtful. Frustrated. Ugly. Scorned. Now imagine an enviable woman boasting her success with Nice Guys at a wild party or in a neighborhood bookstore, and tell me you wouldn't want to knock her right off that self-righteous pedestal. The last thing we want is for that enviable persona to be you.

 WARNING: Should you recognize a BBA in need, trust that it's your responsibility to reach out.

BBAs know that knee-high boots speak louder than words. But guess what? Actions do too. The best way to encourage Bad Boy fanatics is through example.

Nothing touches a BBA's heart more than a legit couple in love. A potential BBA may seem like a standard-free flirt on the outside—but like you, she simply wants a worthy man to want her back. As a recovered BBA and your Nice Guy's better half, practicing the 12 principles in every situation (from lunch dates to work events) will help set an example that others will be drawn to follow.

Can You Handle the Truth?

I think you can. I think that after weeks of confessions and inventory and guidance, you know yourself a hell of a lot better than you like to admit. In fact, I think you can deal very nicely with the truth behind why you were able to convert so seamlessly to the Nice Guy agenda.

Are you sitting down? Stroking Lolita? Eating those strawberries? Brilliant.

Because here's the secret to your success: Deep down inside, you've got more than a hint of Good Girl tucked away for safe keeping. Oh, yes you do! And it's nothing to be ashamed of. Not one bit. Look at yourself! You're basking in the attention, respect, and love of a deserving young thing—and you don't even miss the allure of a wounded diversion. You might hanker for a hunka forearm every once in a while, but it's nothing your Nice Guy can't define at the gym. And you see that now, primarily because it takes a closeted Good Girl—with pure intentions and a strong will—to fall for a Nice Guy. Your lovable self might have been buried under years of sardonic dating disaster stories, but that kinder, gentler soul was bound to surface with the right amount of prodding. Major epiphanies don't happen every day, you know. And very seldom do women have more than one, maybe two in a row (unless they're faking it). So embrace the ride you had as a BBA 12-Stepper, and realize that you came out the other side a more real version of yourself.

Just because I don't recommend throwing your success in another BBA's face does not mean that you shouldn't celebrate with your Sponsor, Higher Power, friends, boyfriend, and family! You have so much to appreciate now—and a lot of people to thank for holding your hand along the way. New friends, new interests, and a new definition of sex appeal are among your praiseworthy perks. At the very least, throw yourself the most uncivilized party you can choreograph—with a guest list that proves your new cohorts can mingle with old and that Nice can mix with reformed or platonic Bad. Fruity cocktails, riotous guests, and wicked party favors will pull every detail together. Ask your Nice Guy to jump out of a cake! Set up a kissing booth to thank your Sponsor! Beat a Bad Boy piñata filled with licorice whips, Red Hots, and Jawbreakers! Much like your dating life now, the party possibilities are endless.

Not Every Nice Guy Finishes First

On rare occasions, you may wonder—if just for a minute—if your recovered BBA status is overrated. This will most likely occur when you're playing wingman to a boy-crazy friend or receiving a wink from the disheveled bartender at your new favorite lounge. Don't overanalyze, but do see each situation for its reality: Your girlfriend will expend more energy pleasing any Bad Boy she dates than he will pleasing her, and the gnarly bartender hasn't used conditioner in days. (Imagine what his pillow cases smell like? Gross.) Believe me, you're better off.

Now and then, you may also wonder if your Nice Guy is The One for you. This is obviously something I can't answer since we've regrettably never met, but you've done enough self-evaluating to at least know what's important to you in a relationship. What makes you happy? What are your priorities now—and what does your frame look like for the future? No Nice Guy can be your everything, but if you don't feel satiated or compatible in important lifestyle categories (only you know what they are), then don't settle with this one either. You've mingled with enough men, Good and Bad, to know how each affects you. Sometimes, your first Nice Guy is simply a running start—and that's nothing to regret, because you now know more clearly what you're looking for in a mate. Of course, Nice Guys are harder to break up with than Bad Boys because they're such wonderful people and have invested so much in your well-being. If D-Day does arrive, though, stay positive, honest, and full of love. Cry, then cry some more. You'll be surprised at how much you mean it when you ask him if you two can still be friends.

 WARNING: Sometimes, your first Nice Guy is simply a running start—and that's nothing to regret, because you now know more clearly what you're looking for in a mate.

Although you've softened considerably, don't file down every pointy edge. As you shake your BBA inclinations, unexpected elements of your persona may emerge that you might not recognize. You may become more silly, less candid, more personable, less sarcastic—and these are all good things because they indicate change for the better. But you do want to hold on to a little badass. It would be pretty lame to chuck your entire identity just because you're dating new types of men. Plus, it's important to keep the caustic radar up so you can ward off shaky scenarios with sharp intuition. Circumstances that might prove confusing—say, trying to suss out the difference between a Bad Boy and a Good Boy Behaving Badly— may require a cautious Q&A, with one eyebrow cocked and an undermining tone. Within three minutes of your snarky inquisition, you'll have an answer much faster than your amicable self would. With the right voice and mannerisms, a man's reaction to a simple question like, "Did your Mom knit you that scarf?" could yield a more accurate read than a crystal ball.

When Life Hands You Rotten Bananas . . .

As I racked my head for a happy ending anecdote to wrap this chapter, my friend Alia called with the best Nice Guy anecdote I'd heard in weeks, years, eons! After three months of gallivanting about with a Nice Guy, Alia made him muffins from old bananas she'd salvaged from his kitchen the previous weekend. And while the cakes were still warm, she messengered them to his office. Her attached note said: "I don't ever pay for dinner, but sometimes I do steal rotting fruit from men's kitchen tables and bake things with it." His response? "Wow. It's been a long time since a woman's baked me anything. . . . "

The transaction made Alia realize that her Nice Guy, unlike most Bad Boys she's dated, is a Giver. "And I think most modern women are conditioned to be Takers," she said. "I'm not sure when this happened, exactly. Maybe we're playing into traditional provider/provided-for roles? Or maybe we all read *The Rules* too closely in the '90s?" Regardless, Alia concluded there was something about dating Bad Boys that made her cautious about fully opening up to show off her endearing best (e.g., *Why bother making him a card, when you know it will end up in the recycle bin?*). But with Nice Guys, Alia noticed that, "being around one actually makes me want to be nice back. Nice Guys cultivate compassion, which says a lot coming from this jaded, over-intellectualized urbanite. And that can't be a bad thing."

So there you have it. Dating a Nice Guy is hardly a humanitarian effort. But it does remind you of how powerful and satisfying it feels to *want* to make someone else smile—and how much it matters to everyone when you do.

ALIA'S BANANA MUFFIN RECIPE

Isn't it amazing to know you can turn something so bruised and rotten like an old banana into something so warm and tasty like a fresh-baked muffin? Similarly, BBAs use old experiences to inform new ones. Imagine the possibilities when you combine cruddy encounters with a heap of your fresh point of view to reinvent a yummy new life! Now that's a delicious metaphor.

1. Begin with all ingredients at room temperature. Position a rack in the lower third of the oven; preheat to 350°F.

2. Whisk together:

   1⅓ cups all-purpose flour

   ¾ teaspoon salt

   ½ teaspoon baking soda

   ¼ teaspoon baking powder

3. In a large bowl, beat on high speed for two minutes, until light in color and texture:

   5⅓ tablespoons unsalted butter

   ⅔ cup brown sugar

4. Beat in flour mixture until blended. Gradually beat in:

   2 large eggs

5. Fold in, just until combined:

½ cup chopped pecans

¼ cup chocolate chips

*1 cup of mashed, very ripe bananas (about two), prefer-
ably rescued from your Nice Guy's Philippe Starck fruit bowl
where they were left for dead in the pristine stainless steel
kitchen he never uses.*

6. Muffin pans should be greased or lined with paper cups, if
you want to be cute about it. Grease the top of the pan to
make giant muffins with mushrooming tops. Nonstick spray
is easiest to use, but if you prefer a buttery taste, go crazy
with a stick of the yellow stuff.

7. Fill muffin cups to any level you wish. The standard muffin
requires about ⅔ full, but you can fill cups to the rim or even
heap the batter over the rim for giant muffins.

8. Baking times vary according to the size of the muffin pan: A
mini muffin will take 10–12 minutes; a standard-sized muffin, 15–18 minutes; and a jumbo muffin, 22–25 minutes.

9. Enjoy! Enjoy!

Afterword

Take Back the Nice!

My mother is a high school English teacher. Which may (or may not) explain why she reprimanded me for using the word "nice" as a child, when other kids received wrist slaps for sneaking Oreos before dinner. "Nice is an empty word," she would say. "The English language has given us rich adjectives to better describe a person, place, or thing. Nice is almost as empty as 'good.'"

Though Mom's lesson worked magic on my SAT scores, it didn't do a damn thing for my love life. And if I were the type to blame all lousy circumstances on my upbringing, I might even point to this anecdote as the reason why I became a BBA in the first place. But the truth is that more people than my mother equate the words "nice" and "good" with "empty"—especially when it comes to men. Nice Guys are adoring, generous, loving, gentle—and, some might even say, life changing. And as a recovering addickt who's mad about Nice Guys, I feel it's my civil duty to call bullshit on this theory. Care to join me?

That's my girl. It's time to Take Back the Nice! We can't allow ourselves to be victimized by someone else's definition of what it means to date cute, date smart, and date up. We must speak as a unified voice against social dictates that condition us to believe the unbelievable: That men who are inaccessible, insensitive, and insane are the ultimate catch. We must debunk the myths of Nice, so we never have to hear our friends complain, "He's just too n---" again. That's like saying microwaves are too convenient or makeup artists are overrated on your wedding day.

So now that you're a recovering BBA, it's my greatest wish that you'll re-enter the dating world as an enthusiastic lover of quality men. And that you truly believe Nice is not an empty word, but one that promises more fulfillment than any short-term thrill a Bad Boy could promise—and, subsequently, neglect to deliver. If I had the nerve to say these things to Mom twenty years ago, perhaps *ma vie d'amour* would be very different.

Not that I have any regrets. Because my BBA experiences stung like they did, each man's role proved to be an important one; dicey relationships helped me see the good more clearly in valuable men. I can't help but think that it's better to have loved and lost a few Bad Boys, than never to have loved at all. Especially when they're the catalyst to a very Nice reward.

Appendix

Haven't You Had Enough?

Of course not! You may have kicked your Bad Boy habit, but you'll never lose your insatiable appetite for all things new and more. That's why I've collected a few extra tips and tidbits for additional research, growth, and gratification. Share some, and hoard others. What's most important is that you're good and satisfied—so you can finally get out there and show the right men what you've learned.

Bad Versus Good:
A Film, Lit, and Life Reference Guide

To expand your savvy about Bad Boy and Nice Guy archetypes, look no further. The following lists spotlight what we love to hate, and hate to love, about beaux past and present.

Film: Exposing the Bad Boy

○ Alfie

○ American Psycho

○ Blow

○ Casablanca

○ Chaplin

○ Citizen Kane

○ Dangerous Liaisons

○ Dog Day Afternoon

○ Fight Club

○ Goodfellas

○ Heathers

○ In the Company of Men

○ Less Than Zero

○ Mean Streets

○ Rodger Dodger

○ Scream

○ Taxi Driver

○ Training Day

○ Trainspotting

○ Wonderland

Film: Praising the Nice Guy

○ 13 Going on 30

○ The 40-Year-Old Virgin

○ After Hours

○ Along Came Polly

○ The Baxter

○ Bridget Jones's Diary

○ Can't Buy Me Love

○ Can't Hardly Wait

○ Clueless

○ Desperately Seeking Susan

○ Edward Scissorhands

○ Flirting

○ Legally Blonde

○ Little Shop of Horrors

○ Notting Hill

○ Say Anything

○ Sleepless in Seattle

○ Something Wild

○ The Wedding Singer

○ When a Man Loves a Woman

Literary Figures: Exposing the Bad Boy

DRACULA: If a guy makes you change that much for him, he's not worth it.

FRANKENSTEIN: It's a bad sign when he spends more time with his unholy creature than with you.

HAMLET: Most Bad Boys figuratively drive a girl crazy. This one did it for real.

HEATHCLIFF, FROM *WUTHERING HEIGHTS*: Man, could this dude hold a grudge.

SIR LANCELOT: Slick Lance stole Queen Guinevere's heart—and then got them both banished.

NARCISSUS: It's all in his name.

ROBIN HOOD: If he really loved Maid Marian, he would have stopped sleeping in the forest and found himself a real job.

ROMEO: Romance, schmomance. If you end up dead, the relationship's not a good one.

TOM SAWYER: He loses Becky in a cave and convinces her he's dead. Hello, commitment issues.

THE WHITE RABBIT, FROM *ALICE IN WONDERLAND*: He ran, she chased— and she almost lost her head because of it. There's a lesson here, ladies. . . .

Literary Figures: Praising the Nice Guy

CYRANO DE BERGERAC: What a faithful friend! And you know what they say about the size of a man's nose. . . .

MR. DARCY, FROM *PRIDE AND PREJUDICE*: Proof that Nice Guys can look hot in a wet shirt, too.

THE DUKE, FROM *TWELFTH NIGHT*: When a straight man falls for a woman pretending to be a guy, you have to believe his feelings are legit.

FRED, FROM *BREAKFAST AT TIFFANY'S*: Fred was gay, but the good ones often are. Hollywood renewed our faith with a little character tweak. . . .

THE FROG PRINCE: What charm! What grace! Then again, being trapped for years as an amphibian is a great way to learn manners.

KING ARTHUR: He gave his woman everything, and then lost her and the war in return. Nobody said Nice Guys always finish first. . . .

MARCUS, FROM *LES MISERABLES*: Hey, he said he was Cosette's man from day one. You can't blame the Eponine fiasco on him.

NED NICKERSON, FROM *NANCY DREW*: Aah, to be young, in love, and solving the mystery of Crocodile Island. . . . Now that's partnership.

ODYSSEUS: He spent 10 years finding his way back to his true love. Most would have given it a week.

PRINCE CHARMING: There's a reason so many are still looking for him.

Historical Figures: Exposing the Bad Boy

ATTILA THE HUN: You know your man's avoiding quality time at home when he runs off to invade Europe.

NAPOLEON BONAPARTE: He'd say he was gone, but he kept coming back.

CALIGULA: Even if he were to say you're the one, Saturday nights were always about the orgy.

BILL CLINTON: It's bad enough that he smokes cigars. . . .

GANDHI: Sure he wouldn't beat you up, but he'd always make you feel fat by comparison.

HENRY VIII: He's worse than Billy Bob Thornton when it came to nixing ex-wives.

ADOLF HITLER: Ask Eva Braun if that relationship ended well.

HOWARD HUGHES: We don't like that he slept around, but who could build a meaningful relationship with a man who collects jars of his own pee?

THOMAS JEFFERSON: The founding father—to a whole bunch of racially diverse babies.

PLATO: Instead of dinner at home, he insisted on hanging with the boys . . . the very young boys.

VINCENT VAN GOGH: Hey, V.G. Try harder than cutting off an ear to impress a woman. **SEE ABELARD.**

Historical Figures: Praising the Nice Guy

ABELARD: A medieval monk who made the ultimate sacrifice for Heloise: his testicles.

JOHN ADAMS: He valued his wife's opinion on running the country and ignored presidential matters to be by her side when sick. Not great for the United States, but pretty nice for the Mrs.

ROBERT BROWNING: He fell in love with his future wife Elizabeth through her poetry and encouraged her to leave her room for the first time in years. How a rich heiress and internationally famous literary figure ever inspired such devotion, we'll never know. . . .

WINSTON CHURCHILL: Despite the bombing of London, he always had time for his family.

JESUS: A woman doesn't wash a man's feet for nothing.

ABE LINCOLN: He freed the slaves and still had time to take his best girl to a show.

PAUL NEWMAN: The couple that makes salad dressing together, stays together.

PRINCE ALBERT: Queen Victoria's main squeeze was both strong and supportive. He really didn't deserve to have a penis piercing named in his honor.

CHRÉSTIEN DE TROYES: Authored the Arthurian Romances that helped popularize chivalry. The next time a guy pulls out your chair, thank Chréstien.

Bad Versus Good: Navigating Your Journey

Once you've accepted your BBA status, extra encouragement during recovery is always welcome. Especially when it includes a mix of sex tips, Mom's quips, and boring drips. . . .

Why Your Nice Guy Will Excel at Bad Boy Sex

BONDAGE: He won't tie you up and then go on a beer run. Plus, he'll honor the safe word.

DIRTY TALK: He'll whisper tawdry eroticisms in your ear, and he won't fantasize about doing them with his #1 Hooter's waitress.

EROTIC MASSAGE: He'll dig into tired muscles with strong fingers—and wait longer than 30 seconds before demanding some action.

PDA: His idea of PDA does not involve grabbing your boob at the office picnic.

PHONE SEX: He won't call collect.

SEX TOYS: He can fix them if they break.

STRIP TEASE: As you swivel your hips in a thong, he won't unfavorably compare you to Chrystal from Scores—and then hire Chrystal as your personal coach.

Maternal Wisdom: A Letter from My Mom

Dear Readers,

The only thing worse than being an addickt is being the mother of an addickt. I know a BBA's plight is a rough one, but believe me: It's nothing compared to what your parents have been through with you. Try to suspend your disbelief for just a minute. . . .

Imagine having a young, single, vulnerable daughter who lives all by herself. Your phone rings at 2 A.M., your heart pounds—and you expect to hear the controlled voice of an SVU squad member on the line. Instead, you hear the voice of a little girl who, between sobs, tells you that she just learned that her boyfriend of three months screwed some slutty blonde he met at a work party.

I remember when this happened to Kristina. I tried to comfort her by calling the guy a slimy bastard. But I really wanted to ask her, "What did you expect?" Smoldering, hypnotic, charismatic types who seduce with empty words and big schlongs are good for one-night-stands but nothing else. They're often handsome, extremely virile, and very persuasive. Bad Boys make women feel sexy, needed, and important—but they can also make them feel used, worthless, and disposable. And as tortured souls, these creeps carry more baggage than a family on holiday.

Long-lasting relationships happen with men who are loving as well as loyal; interesting as well as functional. Nice Guys have their feet on the ground, not their head in the clouds. Yet with each of Kristina's Bad Boy relationships, all I could do was listen to my daughter work through her latest upset. After countless hours of self-reflection and validation, I'd hope for a few uninterrupted nights—until the next Bad Boy Svengali came along. When she finally met a genuine Nice Guy, I was happy for her and for myself. I could finally get some sleep.

When it comes to finding real love, my advice is to look for a man who's kind, stable, generous to a fault, loves his mother (but not too much), and, most importantly, loves you unconditionally. You'll be thrilled, and you'll stop driving your parents crazy.

Fondly,

Mrs. Grish (Call me Anna)

Yes, There's a Difference Between Nice and Boring

....

A NICE GUY: Designs you a one-of-a-kind necklace.
A BORING BLOKE: Regifts from Mom's junk jewelry collection—and calls the booty an heirloom.

....

A NICE GUY: Makes your bed in the morning.
A BORING BLOKE: Arranges your throw pillows by color, and throws a fit when you move them.

....

A NICE GUY: Feeds you chicken soup when you're sick.
A BORING BLOKE: Hands you antibiotics through a crack in the door, so he's not "contaminated."

....

A NICE GUY: Reads to you from a book of poetry.
A BORING BLOKE: Reads to you from a book of geometry.

....

A NICE GUY: Takes you out dancing.
A BORING BLOKE: Takes you out dancing to Polka Night at the local nursing home.

....

A NICE GUY: Prepares a wonderful meal.
A BORING BLOKE: Prepares a wonderful meal made entirely of bean curd and bamboo shoots.

....

A NICE GUY: Makes sweet, soulful love to you while consulting the *Kama Sutra*.
A BORING BLOKE: Makes fast, awkward love to you while consulting his sixth grade health textbook.

Bad Versus Good: The Aftermath

You've moved on from BBA behavior, so it's time to start fresh! Here, a few final suggestions on what you'll take away from each relationship—and a soundtrack for backup.

Out with the Old, in with the New

....

IF A BAD BOY TOOK YOUR: Best years
THEN YOU SHOULD TAKE HIS: Best Levis

....

IF A BAD BOY TOOK YOUR: Good health
THEN YOU SHOULD TAKE HIS: Good wealth

....

IF A BAD BOY TOOK YOUR: Faith in love
THEN YOU SHOULD TAKE HIS: Faith in locks (Use your extra key wisely. You have friends who would appreciate a new armchair.)

....

IF A BAD BOY TOOK YOUR: TLC and charity
THEN YOU SHOULD TAKE HIS: Toyota Camry and donate it to charity

....

IF A GOOD BOY GIVES YOU: His attention, no matter what the topic
THEN YOU SHOULD GIVE HIM: Feigned interest in action films and the Red Sox

....

IF A GOOD BOY GIVES YOU: Empathy
THEN YOU SHOULD GIVE HIM: MP3s of all the songs that croon how much you care

....

IF A GOOD BOY GIVES YOU: Oral sex for hours
THEN YOU SHOULD GIVE HIM: Whatever he asks for, plus waffles for breakfast

....

IF A GOOD BOY GIVES YOU: TLC and charity
THEN YOU SHOULD GIVE HIM: That Toyota Camry you almost gave to charity

Who's Up for a Mix Tape? Songs to Include, by All Means

○ "50 Ways to Leave Your Lover" (Paul Simon)

○ "Chain of Fools" (Aretha Franklin)

○ "Charmless Man" (Blur)

○ "The Great Escape" (We Are Scientists)

○ "Happy Alone" (Kings of Leon)

○ "Hound Dog" (Elvis Presley)

○ "Hung in a Bad Place" (Oasis)

○ "I'll Be Alright without You" (Journey)

○ "Independent Woman pt. 1" (Destiny's Child)

○ "I Will Survive" (Gloria Gaynor)

○ "I Won't Die Alone" (Shelby Lynne)

○ "Kick" (INXS)

○ "The Power of Goodbye" (Madonna)

○ "Since I Left You" (The Avalanches)

○ "There, There" (Radiohead)

○ "Tired" (Tommy Lee)

○ "Wake Up" (Missy Elliot)

○ "Weirdo" (The Charlatans)

○ "Where Is the Line?" (Björk)

○ "You Ain't Getting None" (Eve)

Who's Up for a Mix Tape? Songs to Avoid, at All Costs

✘ "Aging Spinsters" (The 6ths)

✘ "Bad Boys" (Janet Jackson)

✘ "Come Undone" (Duran Duran)

✘ "Communication Breakdown" (Led Zeppelin)

✘ "The Dangling Conversation" (Simon and Garfunkel)

✘ "Driving Sideways" (Aimee Mann)

✘ "The Drugs Don't Work" (Verve)

✘ "Excuse Me While I Break My Own Heart Tonight" (Whiskey Town)

✘ "Fuck the Pain Away" (Peaches)

✘ "I Can't Make You Love Me" (Bonnie Raitt)

✘ "I Fall to Pieces" (Patsy Cline)

✘ "Keep Me Hanging On" (Kim Wilde)

✘ "Killing Me Softly" (Roberta Flack)

✘ "Nothing Compares 2 U" (Sinead O'Connor)

✘ "One" (U2)

✘ "Panic Attack" (Unkle)

✘ "Pissed Off" (Angie Stone)

✘ "She Don't Love You" (Lil' Kim)

✘ "She's Lost Control" (Joy Division)

✘ "Toxic" (Britney Spears)

photo © Perry Hagopian

About the Author

KRISTINA GRISH is the author of *Boy Vey! The Shiksa's Guide to Dating Jewish Men* and *We Need to Talk. But First, Do You Like My Shoes? Dress Codes for Dumping Your Man*. She recently completed her fourth book, *The Joy of Text: Dating, Mating, and Techno-Relating*. Kristina is a contributing editor to *Marie Claire*, and has written essays and features for *Cosmopolitan*, *Men's Health*, *Teen Vogue*, *Zink*, and *Vibe*, among others. She lives and dates in New York City. Visit her at www.kristinagrish.com.